Environmental Policy and Welfare Economics

Environmental Policy and Welfare Economics

KRISTER HJALTE
KARL LIDGREN
INGEMAR STAHL

Translated by CURT WELLS

CAMBRIDGE UNIVERSITY PRESS

CAMBRIDGE
LONDON · NEW YORK · MELBOURNE

Published by the Syndics of the Cambridge University Press
The Pitt Building, Trumpington Street, Cambridge CB2 1RP
Bentley House, 200 Euston Road, London NW1 2DB
32 East 57th Street, New York, NY 10022, USA
296 Beaconsfield Parade, Middle Park, Melbourne 3206, Australia

First published 1977

Phototypeset by Western Printing Services Ltd, Bristol
and printed in Great Britain by Billing & Sons Ltd
Guildford, London and Worcester

Library of Congress Cataloguing in Publication Data
Hjalte, Krister, 1944–
Environmental policy and welfare economics.
1. Environmental policy. 2. Welfare economics.
I. Lidgren, Karl, 1947– joint author. II. Ståhl,
Ingemar, 1938– joint author. III. Title.
HC79E5H5713 1977 301.31 76–47191
ISBN 0 521 21549 8 hard covers
ISBN 0 521 29182 8 paperback

Contents

1
Environmental policy and welfare economics – an introduction

1.1 The economic aspect

Economics is the study of how society can allocate scarce resources to satisfy human needs. One branch of economic theory studies such aspects of economic life as the production of goods and services and the distribution of the final product among members of society. Another branch is concerned with the institutions and basic organizations within which the various raw materials are transformed into goods and services that can be utilized by individual consumers. Note, however, that neither the raw material nor the final product need be economic in the narrow meaning that it can be measured in dollars and cents, nor need it be distributed via markets where money changes hands.

One must keep in mind this rather broad definition of the economic problem when one analyzes environmental policy and the use of scarce resources such as natural resources and environmental quality. This rather general view of an economic system with regard to the interaction between environmental policy and the economic system will be followed throughout the book. Problems such as how one best can use scarce resources such as water or clean air for recreational purposes must be considered economic problems in the same way that the traditional problems of distribution are.

This approach also implies that the description of man's differing productive activities must be broadened to include those activities that affect the environment. This idea may be illustrated by the simple diagram overleaf.

During a given time period, the production processes use positive inputs of the differing, but limited, supplies of society's capital and labor resources. As the diagram indicates, these processes also require certain natural and environmental resources as inputs. Actually, we can take a further step in this line of reasoning: society's consumers are interested in, not so much the actual commodities, but rather the services that the said commodities render them. One does not consume a refrigerator; one uses the chilled atmosphere it produces to help preserve food. Further, the often used phrase 'final consumption' is actually misleading – material goods do not disappear into a bottomless pit but are returned to nature after the consumer has used the services they provide.

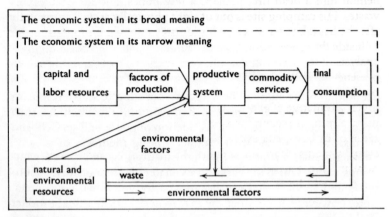

Figure 1

Physically, nothing really disappears – the total mass of all produced goods at every level of production is always equal to the weight of the goods in the earlier stages of production as well as to the weight of the final products plus the by-products. Depending on how tightly controlled the production and consumption processes are, more or less all of the by-products considered as waste materials are returned to their original environment and affect its quality, usually detrimentally.

Thus an analysis of an economic system's capability for solving the economic problem of allocating scarce resources to differing and competing ends must include *both* the flow of natural and environmental resources *into* the production process and the flow of wastes from the production and consumption processes *back to* the natural environment. Equally important are the services that consumers obtain directly from this natural environment. In the diagram, this particular flow is indicated by the arrow from 'natural and environmental resources' to 'final consumption'. The quality of the natural resources directly affects the consumers' standard of living.

But why should the use of natural resources be considered an economic problem and how should an economic organization, capable of guiding production and consumption, be designed to yield desirable results? The following two examples illustrate the problem:[1]

The primitive hunter camps on the plains, lighting a small fire to give him light and momentary warmth. A whisp of smoke trickles up towards the heavens. The following day he breaks camp, leaving behind him a dead fire, perhaps a few bones, and his own bodily wastes. His camping site is out of sight physically as well as mentally after he has taken ten steps on his journey to new hunting grounds.

Inside the space capsule, an instrument panel reports a computer's analysis of its environment: the percentage of oxygen in the air, the presence of poisonous wastes, the amount of fuel in its tanks. The machine also calculates how long the oxygen and the fuel will last given alternative flight patterns. The air in the capsule is recycled using a computer controlled process, the limited supplies of food are rationed by computer order, bodily wastes are collected in ingenious closed systems. Warning signals flash and initiate planned corrective measures if the actual values measured by the computer differ from the planned ones.

These examples illustrate two extreme economies – extreme in the relationship of man to his environment. In the first case, nature is infinite and has an almost infinite capacity to absorb such wastes as are produced: one cannot speak of an environmental problem. Contrast this case with the second one, and where survival is dependent upon the calculations of a machine. Here nothing can be consumed without a careful analysis of this consumption's effect on the next minute or day of the economy's life.

Which of the examples best illustrates our current situation? Are we on our way from the infinite environment of the primitive hunter to the closed space ship world of the second example?

If this is the case, do we possess an intricate control mechanism which corresponds to the capsule's computer, which can provide our economy with the necessary information and control to ensure our survival? Even if our resources are not so scarce as to threaten our physical existence, are our possibilities of controlling the environment sufficiently advanced to ensure a comfortable, or at any rate tolerable existence?

It is, of course, not possible to answer these questions within the

---

[1] The examples presented are modifications of those presented in Kneese, A. V. et al., Economics and the Environment, Material Balance Approach, Washington, DC, 1970.

framework of a book such as this. Our purpose must be limited to that of demonstrating how these problems can be analyzed by using the tools of economic theory. The technical and ecological problems involved will hardly be touched upon. Our discussions will rather be concentrated on explaining how environmental questions can be considered problems of resource allocation and on showing how our institutions and organizations – our control bodies corresponding to the space capsule's computer – can improve our lot.

1.2 The price system and the environment

The price system in a market economy with decision making in production and consumption decentralized is in essence a mechanism for guiding the economy towards an efficient or 'optimal' state. The following passage is intended to illustrate how the price system functions as a control body.

The supply of capital, as well as that of certain natural resources, such as organic fuels and minerals, is, at each moment in time, limited. Those who own these resources sell them or the services they produce to firms. Similarly individuals sell their labor services to these firms via the labor market. The firms buy these services and combine them with differing inputs of the various factors of production to yield combinations of goods and services. It is not unreasonable to assume that each firm will choose the production mix that yields maximum profit. These products are then sold either to other firms as semi-manufactured goods or to consumers for final consumption. The consumers receive their income from the services they sell to the firm. Here it is reasonable to assume that the consumers will choose the best available combination of goods – that which they value the greatest – given their income and the current prices. In the next chapter we shall demonstrate that, under certain conditions, there exists a set of prices that will guide the economy to an efficient production as well as to an efficient consumption position and, at the same time, to an equilibrium state where demand and supply are equal in each and every market.

In an economy with millions of consumers and firms and tens of thousands of commodities, the main service that the price system performs is to act as a guide for decentralized control. The price of any given commodity depends not only on consumer preferences but also on the relative scarcity of the good or of those resources used in producing it. If the supply of a certain raw material decreases, its price will increase and its use will decrease both in direct consumption and in the productive processes. A new equilibrium price that corresponds to the new demand and supply conditions will be established.

It is often extremely difficult to foresee all of the consequences of a given decrease (increase) in supply and resulting increase (decrease) in the price of a given raw material. Once a new equilibrium is established, one will find that not only has the price of the particular raw material increased, but that the prices of many other, if not all, raw materials and commodities will also have changed. The discovery of a new oil field and the resultant increase in supply and decrease in price will imply, among other things, lower costs for heating homes: the same room temperature can now be maintained at a lower cost. Or conversely, a lower quality of insulation will not result in higher heating bills. While home owners see their heating bills decreasing, the building industry will see less reason to consider heating costs in new construction and will tend to produce large, poorly insulated houses. Lower oil prices lead to cheaper gasoline and thus to an increase in motoring. Further, the motor industry will find demand for the smaller models to be decreasing relative to that for the larger ones. Heavier cars with a higher gasoline consumption will result. This change will also be noted by those industries that deliver semi-finished goods to the auto industry: the demand for steel will rise, as will that industry's demand for fuel. Finally, we note that the demand for (and therefore the price of) other sources of energy – such as water power and atomic energy – will also be affected.

Thus the price system in a market economy is an instrument through which information on changes in raw material supplies can be spread throughout the economy. Standard textbooks in economics are, however, quick to point out that various market imperfections hinder the effectiveness of the price system in its role as a distributor of information. Monopolized industries, the price regulations that many governments seemingly enjoy imposing, and the varying rates at which prices adjust to changing conditions are usually cited as examples. However, in the discussion of environmental policy, one can disregard many of these imperfections: conservation of the environment is not intimately connected with monopolies, their price setting and their profits. That a market economy can exhibit both unemployment and a polluted environment does not necessarily imply that both of these ills have the same cause: these problems are normally quite independent of each other.

The reason why the price system in a market economy functions less than perfectly with respect to environmental issues is that it covers only a limited number of natural resources. A firm that emits sulphur dioxide into the atmosphere is using a scarce resource (the atmosphere) in its production process and changes it via this process to a resource of lower quality. Consumers who value clean air find that their standard of living has decreased. Other firms that are dependent on the input of clean air in their production find that their productivity has decreased and/or their costs have increased. Firms or households that discharge their sewage directly into a river reduce downstream water quality. This reduction in turn lowers the recreational value of the river and can force firms located downstream (which are dependent on clean water for their production) to install water purifying plants.

Cars that emit lead compounds in their exhausts can cause an increase in the lead content of crops growing near the road, and, indirectly lead to the accumulation of lead in animal and human bodies. Not only does the motorist use the road but also by emitting exhaust fumes he affects the quality of a product such as grain growing along the roadside.

A further example of how the market price may communicate incomplete information is provided by a fisherman. As he increases his catch from a given (and limited) stock of fish, he increases costs (or reduces the revenues) of others who fish in the same area. As the individual fisherman can never be sure that he will catch at some future time the fish that he throws back into the water today, he has no incentive to throw it back. Uncoordinated fishing thus leads individuals to underestimate the true costs of their actions: the greater today's catch for the individual, the smaller the catch and the greater the cost of fishing for all fishermen tomorrow.

A beer bottle discarded in the forest does indeed disappear from sight and mind for the person who left it there after a few steps – but this act is not comparable to our primitive hunter's dead camp fire. Others who enjoy the forest find their pleasure reduced as they stumble over such discarded relics of our civilization. The cost of leaving the bottle in the forest is the decrease in the forest's recreational value to those who visit it. No one sends the firm a bill for the clean air it uses in its production processes; the water in the river has no listed market price; the farmer cannot bill passing motorists for their negative contributions to his crops; there is no agency that owns the fish in the sea and can charge the fishermen the true cost of their catch; and the land owner (or the next camper) has little chance of charging those littering his property (or the camp site) for the damage done. If the price system is to function effectively, it must encompass all of the factors of production and the products of a given production process. Many if not all environmental problems are due to a breakdown in the price system: for one reason or another, it fails to convey a message about the relative scarcity of environmental resources to the users of these resources; the price system does not reflect the opportunity cost of these resources to present or future firms or consumers.

1.3 The environment and externalities

There are several theoretical approaches to the issues outlined above. The classic approach follows that of the English economist Pigou's work during the 1920s, and evolves around a discussion of *externalities*. In an economic context, an externality is said to exist when one firm's production (or an individual's consumption) affects the production process (or standard of living) of another firm (or individual) in the absence of market transactions between them. The factory emitting smoke into the atmosphere or sewage directly into a river is an example of a *negative* externality: other firms dependent upon clean air or water are directly injured by the factory's production processes. The bather leaving his beer cans on the beach is a further example: his actions affect directly and adversely the pleasure of future sunbathers.

Externalities can, of course, be positive as well as negative. One can easily conceive of situations where one firm's production increases the production of another firm. The example of the beekeeper and the apple farmer is a standard one: the bees increase the orchard's crop. A second example of a positive externality would be a home owner who keeps his yard tidy: this improves his neighbor's standard of living.

The theory of externalities can also be expressed in terms of those costs incurred by a certain production process that are internal to a firm and those that are borne by society as a whole. One emphasizes the difference between the costs that the individual producer or consumer bears, and the total costs to society which include costs external to the individual economic unit; that is, one distinguishes between private and social costs. The firm which dumps raw sewage into a river does so in order to minimize its private costs: that the downstream fisherman must increase his costs to maintain an unchanged catch is external to the firm and thus not its concern. As certain resources such as 'clean air' or 'pure water' have no market price the private cost of using these resources will be less than the social cost. If the firm had attempted to minimize social costs it would have chosen a production technique that would have resulted in less damage to the environment. The firm would perhaps have processed its sewage before dumping it in the river, or it might have reduced production. The way to minimize social costs varies from case to case.

Many, or perhaps most of the environmental issues that have been discussed in the past few years can be analyzed in terms of externalities or in terms of the price system's failure to convey correct information about a resource's relative scarcity. But we would like to ask a further question: why does the price system fail to reflect the 'correct' value of so many of our environmental resources? Why do externalities exist? While it is impossible to give a complete answer to these questions, one can indicate the direction in which the answer lies. To begin with, the very operation of a market system implies certain costs. And a condition for a smoothly functioning price system is some form of ownership of, or control over, all the resources in the economy. Compared to other natural resources like oil, ore or timber, environmental resources such as air or water have extremely large, perhaps prohibitive, 'market costs' – that is, those costs necessary to establish ownership or a working price system. As we shall see later, many of the environmental policy instruments can be discussed in terms of whether or not it is possible to reduce or to avoid such 'market costs'.

As long as the environmental problem is of a limited or marginal nature, the theory of externalities, which indicates how adjustments at the margin can improve social efficiency, is a powerful tool of analysis. But in recent years, ecologists have questioned this approach to the problem and have maintained that the problem is so far-reaching that a reconsideration of the economic system and the role of the price system is necessary. The question of how far the environmental problem or the presence of externalities reduces the effectiveness of the economic system is rather controversial, and comprehensive empirical studies are lacking. Can relatively marginal measures – either in the form of taxes on polluting activities or subsidies for sewage treatment or direct regulation of waste discharge or of certain productive activities – be sufficient to allow some form of optimal social choice between the environment and other goods to be made? Or is the environmental problem so all-encompassing that, in the long run, our very existence is seriously threatened, and that a new form of decision making must be found if

.future generations are to have a comfortable standard of living? There is no final answer to these questions, and this work will not attempt to find one. However, we shall discuss the methods through which an answer can be approached. Indeed, the purpose of this work is to lay the ground for a fruitful discussion of these problems. This book will also suggest different means of bringing environmental problems under public control.

1.4 The environment and production

In order to illustrate the nature of the problem in the use of different instruments, we present the schematic representation in figure 2 of the path harmful substances may take on the way to the consumer. A study of the production chain also indicates the nature of the different devices that can be used in environmental policy. The most elegant solution, but also one of the most difficult to implement (and, as a result, a decisive factor in creating today's environmental problems), is to establish ownership over and prices for all environmental resources. In other words, if these resources were incorporated into the economic system many of the problems would be solved. But the very costs of such an incorporation lead to differences between social and private costs.

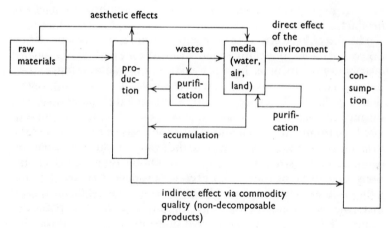

Figure 2 Environmental effects in the production chain.

A broad category of methods is that based on setting taxes or subsidies on wastes, or on activities at an early stage in the production chain in order to provide economic incentives leading to a 'second best' solution. Just how far back in the chain one can go depends largely on administrative costs. In general, a tax is more effective as a control device the closer one comes to the environmental medium. However, as one approaches an ideal method of control, administrative costs tend to increase rapidly. In chapter three we show how this 'proxy' price setting can take an abundance of forms. The discussion of the level of phosphates in detergents, sulphur in oil, or lead in gasoline indicates the nature of the problem; it is impossible to bill the producers directly for the deterioration in the quality of the water, air, or land that is contaminated with these products. Their effect often occurs a great distance in time or space from the actual point of emission. It is a bit easier to collect the tax at the source of the emission – one can base it on the value of the expected damage. However, one can go further back in the production chain and tax the products which actually cause the damage to the environment – that is to say, place taxes on phosphates, on sulphur, or the lead additives.

An alternative to the above two methods is that of direct regulation. Instead of levying a tax on a certain polluting process, one can limit the total amount of the emission. Such directives that forbid certain processes and establish mandatory processing of wastes are measures that affect earlier phases of the production chain. Finally, some regulations limit the amount of certain substances in final products.

The choice between regulation and taxation is mainly a matter of the cost of the administrative controls and the measure's effect on the distribution of income. In many instances the administrative and policing costs of the taxation system are lower than those connected with regulation. Likewise, the implication of the taxation system for income distribution is favorable to those who enjoy an unpolluted environment: this method shifts the costs of protection from the consumer of the environment to the producers and consumers of products that destroy the environment. On the other hand, regulations tend to favor those who produce products that are harmful either in themselves or through the process creating them. In this case, the producers receive what might be termed a 'pollution bonus'. These issues are considered in detail in chapter three.

1.5 The environment, welfare, and the GNP

An individual's welfare is dependent upon those goods and services he consumes as well as intangibles such as environmental quality.

The traditional measures of welfare consider only those commodities that are bought or sold via established markets or provided by governmental agencies. The gross national product – the value of all services and goods produced by society during a given period – is commonly used to measure a country's welfare.

One could, of course, include in the GNP the value of differing 'environmental services', or at least their change in value during the year, thereby creating a more exact measure of welfare. But the task of assigning such values is difficult, if not impossible. In practice, we find that the choice lies between an increase in the quantity of goods and services produced and a corresponding decrease in environmental quality. An improvement in the latter implies all too often a decrease in welfare measured in traditional terms. However, there is no basic conflict between economic welfare in the broad meaning of the term and environmental care; on the contrary, the basic economic problem we face is how the consumer can find some optimal balance between the two.

Figure 3 illustrates the situation. Given the present level of technology, a society's production possibilities can be described by a curve showing the different combinations of goods and services on the one hand, and of environmental quality on the other. As the discussion above indicated, an increase in goods and services from q_1 to q_2 results in a poorer environment, here measured from k_1 to k_2.

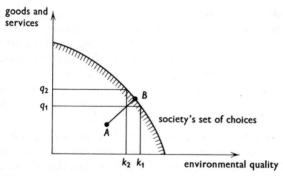

Figure 3 The choice between goods and services and environmental quality.

It should, however, be pointed out that the choice is often much simpler: production in one sector can have a negative influence on that in another sector. Because of the lack of communication between sectors and because of these negative externalities, the total volume of production as well as the environmental quality is *lower* than it would be if the one sector took into consideration its effect on the other. Thus an effective environmental policy can in such cases result in a greater production volume as well as an improved environment. A simple example would be a factory that dumped its wastes directly into a river, thus increasing the water purification costs for those firms on the river dependent upon clean water for their production. This increase in costs can well be in excess of the cost of treating the wastes at the source of pollution. In figure 3, this case is illustrated by a movement from A to B. Point A represents an inefficient use of resources, as it is possible to increase total production without decreasing environmental quality if the factory processed its waste material before dumping it into the river.

2
Allocation, welfare, and environmental policy

Before beginning our economic analysis of environmental problems, we must first briefly familiarize the reader with the theoretical tools we shall use. The presentation here is not intended to be comprehensive; rather it will attempt to present the relevant points in economic theory to the non-professional reader, and it can serve as a review for the economist. We shall cover such broad topics as allocation theory and welfare economics. As we pointed out in chapter one, many of today's environmental problems can be analyzed as different forms of market imperfections or as differences between private and social costs: that is to say, cases where the market economy alone cannot obtain optimal resource allocation. It is thus natural to begin this chapter by presenting the welfare theoretic basis of social efficiency calculations. This presentation is followed by a description of a perfect market economy, whereafter follows a study of those concepts in economic theory more directly connected with our topic: the theory of public goods and external effects. The next chapter will illustrate how the various concepts introduced here can be applied to actual problems.

2.1 Social efficiency calculations: the theoretical background

2.1.1 Social welfare criteria. A basic requirement for a measure of social welfare is that it should, in some sense, measure the welfare of society as a whole, rather than that of a few individuals or groups of individuals. Indicators of social efficiency are usually derived from modern welfare theory.

We begin by assuming that every individual's welfare can be uniquely determined, and that an index number can be assigned to every person's level of utility or welfare. In general, such an index will depend upon the individual's present and future consumption and his assessment of the environment quality variables which cannot be bought or sold on a market. However, this index may also depend on other individuals' standards of living. It is reasonable to require that a measure of social welfare should be based upon the welfare of each and every member of that society. But such functions cannot be derived from decision rules such as majority voting, as the following simple example shows.

Let a society consist of three persons – Adam, Bertil, and Caesar. Further, assume this society shall choose which of three alternative policies alpha, beta, or gamma shall be adopted. Adam prefers this situation in the order given above – that is, alpha gives him the highest utility and gamma the lowest. If both of the other members of society have the same preference structure, then a decision can easily be reached by majority voting. But if they do not have identical preferences, a problem arises. Assume that this is indeed the case, and that their preferences are as presented in the table below.

Adam	*Bertil*	*Caesar*
alpha	beta	gamma
beta	gamma	alpha
gamma	alpha	beta

Let us assume that no coalitions are formed, and that each person votes according to his true preferences. The vote between alpha and beta results in a victory for alpha, as both Adam and Caesar prefer this situation to beta. Similarly, the vote between beta and gamma indicates that society, by a three to two margin, prefers beta. So alpha is preferred to beta and beta is preferred to gamma, we therefore might reasonably require our social welfare function to show alpha is preferred to gamma. Then the preferences between each pair of policies would be consistent. But an examination of the preferences indicates that majority voting would lead to gamma being preferred to alpha. We conclude that a consistent welfare index cannot be based upon majority rule.

There are two ways out of this dilemma: we can either allow one individual to rule for the group as a whole or abandon our attempt to construct a consistent index covering all situations and settle for one covering only some of the possible situations. Both of these possibilities deserve closer attention.

2.1.2 A political welfare function. The first alternative leads to the construction of a consistent welfare function by simply weighting each individual's preferences. This function will obviously reflect the ruling person's or party's preferences and will avoid the problems connected with more complicated decision processes. For example, such a weighting process can be used by a ruling party to establish alpha as superior to gamma in spite of Caesar's dissent.

2.1.3 The Pareto criterion. The second approach could be utilized by considering only those situations which represent an improvement (an increase in welfare, compared to some initial situation) for at least one individual while, at the same time, not worsening any other person's position. This type of social welfare index is usually associated with the Pareto criterion for social changes. This criterion, named after the Italian sociologist and economist Vilfredo Pareto (1848–1923), can be stated as follows: a movement from one situation to another improves social welfare only if no individual receives lower utility from the new situation and at least one person receives greater utility. Changes that satisfy this criterion are called Pareto approved changes. Its advantage is that it serves as a common denominator for a great many different preferences. Suggested changes that satisfy the criterion are attractive, since one expects these to be supported by a rather large portion of society. Figure 4 illustrates the above argument.

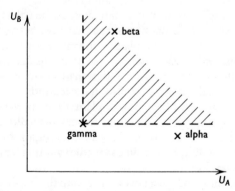

Figure 4 The Pareto criterion.

In figure 4, Adam's and Bertil's welfare indexes, U_A and U_B, have been placed on the horizontal and vertical axis, respectively. Assume that gamma is the initial situation. Alternative beta gives both individuals greater utility: a movement from gamma to beta is thus Pareto sanctioned. This change will have a good chance of being adopted by many different types of social decision processes. Contrast this change to the shift from gamma to alpha. Here Adam's utility increases while Bertil's decreases: the Pareto criterion cannot rank alpha and beta, since the basic requirement of the criterion – that no one receives lower utility – is not fulfilled. The political welfare function could, however, resolve this problem by simply stating that, for example, alpha yields society as a whole greater utility than gamma.

2.1.4 Compensation. There is, however, a way to solve this last mentioned problem within the context of the Pareto criterion: namely, if the 'winners' have the opportunity to compensate the 'losers'. If this *compensation principle* is to be strictly valid, the losers must in fact be compensated. This principle is especially interesting when the compensation takes the form of transfers between individuals. In this case, the condition necessary for a Pareto approved change is that the winners can pay the losers – either in cash or commodities – enough to raise their utility level at least to that of the initial situation.

This rather complicated argument can easily be illustrated with a somewhat oversimplified example. One alternative, delta, implies that a certain river is kept in its original state with accompanying underemployment in the area. Another alternative, epsilon, implies that a hydroelectric power plant is built in the valley. This alternative implies a decrease in environmental quality as the once free-flowing river is now tamed by a dam. Assume that delta is the initial situation. The construction of the plant – alternative epsilon – is Pareto approved if and only if the losers can be compensated in such a way that they maintain the utility level they had in situation delta. The social efficiency calculations require that each individual who considers the construction of the power plant a rape of nature be asked how much he would be willing to pay to keep the valley in its natural state. Similarly, all of the unemployed in the region must be asked how much they would require in payment if alternative delta instead of epsilon were chosen.

If it were possible to levy a tax on the group that wishes to retain an unchanged environment and use the revenue thus obtained to compensate in full the unemployed, alternative delta should be adopted if the tax revenue created was at least equal to compensation. Naturally, if there were other groups that would benefit from the dam construction, such as land owners who would receive a land rent from their property or households who could buy electricity cheaper, they would also need to be compensated from the tax revenues. If, on the other hand, those benefiting from situation epsilon can more than compensate those benefiting from delta – that is, if there is a surplus of funds after the nature lovers have been compensated – then epsilon should be chosen.

The above reasoning uses the Pareto criterion in its strictest sense: those who receive lower utility must actually be compensated so that at least one person gains when society chooses one plan of action instead of another.

2.1.5 Compensation, taxes, and the distribution of income. A strict interpretation of the Pareto criterion is seldom employed. Such an interpretation requires the levying of lump sum taxes and transfers which is hardly feasible given our current tax system which is based mainly on proportional commodities taxes (VAT) and on proportional and progressive income taxes. This then leads us to consider *potential* rather than *actual* compensation in connection with calculations of social efficiency. Potential compensation implies a neutrality in income distribution: a penny gained by one individual is worth as much to the person who lost it. Thus the potential efficiency of any project can be determined by simply summing the losses and gains and comparing these two sums. If the construction of the dam would increase the incomes of those concerned by $25 million while those wishing to retain the valley in its natural state demand $20 million in compensation, then we can claim that the building of the dam will yield a potential social profit of $5 million.

This neutral attitude towards income distribution, that a penny is considered worth the same amount no matter who earns it, can be understood by considering two facts. First of all, politicians do seem to exhibit this neutrality when considering different policies. Secondly, there are so many changes constantly occurring in society that it is difficult if not impossible to determine the effects of one measure on the distribution of income. If a project proves to have unwanted effects on income distribution, these can be corrected after the fact.

2.1.6 Social vs private economic calculations. As the above implies, there are basic differences between social and the more narrow private economic calculations. The first is that the effect of a certain measure on all individuals concerned is considered. Secondly, efficiency for each individual is calculated using the principle of compensation.

The first of these two differences leads immediately to a problem: how broad a group of individuals should be included in the study? Should even those who are not citizens of the state in question be considered? Should we weigh individuals so that those from countries furthest away receive the least attention? In general, we can only suggest that the relevant group changes from case to case – and any report should include a discussion of which group of individuals are considered.

This type of problem appears in connection with the above example. A river valley that is left in its natural state has value not only to the country's own citizens but also to foreign researchers, especially as the wilderness areas in Europe diminish. Further, it is extremely difficult to employ the Pareto criterion in its strictest sense when different generations are involved, even though complicated theoretical solutions have been worked out.

2.1.7 Who owns nature? One is often confronted with another problem connected with the compensation principle: who owns the environment? An example of this problem is contained in the axiom 'the polluter must pay'. Should a firm that emits sulphur dioxide compensate those who live in its vicinity, or should one assume that the firm has a long-term right to pollute and that those who live nearby should pay the firm to reduce its emissions? The end result will, in many cases, be the same except for a different distribution of wealth. Indeed, the firm can, not without justification, demand subsidies if its original plans were based on the premise that its emissions were permissable. Thus the first phase of a practical environmental policy may well be to reduce non-optimal pollution by subsidies rather than by taxes. Another way out of this dilemma is for the authorities simply to declare that after a certain date, say ten to fifteen years in the future, no firm has a right to pollute, and that all environmental resources will after that date become state property, at least for the purposes of compensation for polluting activities. Only a declaration along these lines can give the axiom 'the polluter must pay' functional meaning.

Many laws concerning the environment are formulated in terms of social benefits and how these should be weighted against private costs. Are these laws then based on an actual or on a potential compensation principle? A careful study will show that the laws are not consistent on these questions, nor do they indicate the basis for calculating compensation. Finally, they are strangely quiet when it comes to questions of future ownership of environmental resources.

2.1.8 The applicability of social efficiency calculations. We shall conclude this section by citing a few examples of the applicability of social efficiency calculations at different *levels* of social planning. At the lowest level, such calculations would be termed *project calculations* where one uses methods typical to business firms' cost–income analysis. However, when such projects are concerned with environmental objects, this analysis, which is often very narrow and strictly financial in character, must be broadened to include costs and incomes that are never embodied in financial flows and thus cannot affect the firms' calculations. Such calculations are needed when one considers projects such as the siting of a new hydroelectric plant where environmental considerations are relevant.

Social efficiency calculations can also be applied to such areas as the reform of the basic structures of society. At this level, one does not really seek quantitative solutions, but rather attempts to create behaviorial rules for organizations to follow to achieve some acceptable level of social efficiency. An example would be the rules that an environmental agency should follow in various situations.

On the even higher level, an attempt could be made to implement the conclusions of welfare economics by trying to organize an entire market for environmental services. Chapter three will present a number of such examples – for example by using effluent charges. Perhaps the most important aspect of calculations at this level is to demonstrate that many environmental policy measures are or can be made Pareto approved.

2.2 Individual behavior, demand, and marginal willingness to pay

This section will briefly present that part of economic theory needed to measure an individual's welfare. First we present an individual's welfare function, and we then go on to demonstrate how one can use an individual's preferences to construct measures that can be employed in efficiency calculations.

2.2.1 The individual's choice. The starting point in our analysis is to assume that there exist certain utility yielding entities – goods and services that the individual can purchase at given prices on a market, and a number of environmental factors that he can do nothing about, but that nonetheless affect his own welfare.[1] Examples of such

---

[1] We ignore here a number of services provided by the government either free or at a price below cost to the individual. Examples are defence, education, health care, etc.

environmental factors are the quality of the air, the view from the kitchen window whether of the neighbor's backyard, or the open sea, and the degree of pollution in the nearest lake suitable for swimming. The following discussion assumes that the sometimes nebulous distinction between marketable and environmental commodities is not a problem: a given individual can always distinguish between the two.

We further assume that an individual can rank all conceivable combinations of goods and environmental factors using the relationship 'at least as good as'. We assume that this relationship is *complete* and *transitive*; meaning that the individual can use it to rank all possible situations, and that this ranking is consistent. Transitivity implies that if the individual finds that a situation A is at least as good as another situation, B, and if B is no worse than a third situation, C, then the individual must rank A as at least as good as C.

In requiring that the relationship describing the individual's preferences be both complete and transitive, we are placing a rather loose meaning on the word rational. If our consumer is a rational one, as defined above, then many actions which seem 'irrational' are found to fit into the pattern of his behavior. For example, if he goes into a restaurant, we require that he can rank all dishes on the menu. If he prefers a hamburger and chips to goulash, and goulash to beef, he must also prefer hamburger and chips to beef. Further, rationality does not preclude the possibility that he prefers herring and red wine to fillet of sole and white wine.

2.2.2 Preferences and indifference curves. It is possible to describe an individual's preferences with a simple diagram (figure 5). Combinations B and C are assumed to give the individual equal utility. If we join all points representing combinations of the two goods that give the consumer the same utility as these two, we get what is commonly called an indifference curve. Note that the commodities on the axis can also be environmental factors. Combination D, which is inferior to both B and C, will lie on an indifference curve lying nearer to the origin. We assume *a priori* that an individual will always prefer a combination consisting of more of all goods to one consisting of less. Thus combination A is definitely preferable to D. Situation B contains more of good 2 and less of good 1 than A: is, then, A or B superior?

To answer this question we need more than the above assumption: we need an assumption of *convexity*. This assumption implies that if we take an average of two given combinations on the same indiffer-

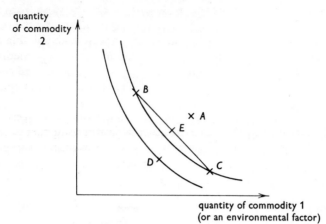

Figure 5 An individual's preferences

ence curve, the resulting combination will not be inferior to the two original ones.[2] For example, if we average B and C, we get combination E. This implies that indifference curves will be convex to the origin.[3] If we then compare E and A, we quickly conclude that the latter is superior. Thus, as E is not inferior to B, we see that A must be superior to B.

Indifference curves may be used to construct a demand curve for marketable goods and the curve representing the marginal willingness to pay for environmental quantities. Figure 6(a) illustrates a typical consumer's choice of consumption. It is assumed that he has a fixed income which he spends entirely on the two commodities and that the market prices of the two goods are given and constant. If he chooses to spend his entire income on commodity 1, he can purchase $\bar{q}$ units of it; similarly, he can choose to consume only $\bar{z}$ units of the other commodity. Any point on the line L_0 represents a consumption expenditure equal to his income: this line is the boundary to the set of possible consumptions. He will choose that consumption in this set which gives him the greatest satisfaction: this occurs at point A where the indifference curve I_2 is tangential to L_0. Points on L_0 to the left and to the right of A are inferior as the consumer would be on a lower indifference curve. For example, point B represents a possible consumption but yields lower utility than A as it lies on an

[2] We assume that a greater quantity of an environmental factor is always preferred to a lesser.
[3] We could also say that all consumptions that are equivalent to or preferred to a certain consumption form a convex sub-set in n-dimensional commodity space.

indifference curve which lies closer to the origin. Thus, z_0 units of 2 and q_0 units of 1 represent the consumer's optimal consumption.

If the price of one of the commodities, say 1, increases, the consumer's real income will decline as the set of possible consumptions will decrease. L_1 in figure 6(a) represents the new budget line, and, again assuming that the consumer spends his entire income on the two goods, his optimal consumption will now be q_1 units of 1, and z_1 units of 2. Figure 6(b) depicts the relationship between the price for a commodity and the quantity demanded when income is kept constant. This demand curve shows that the quantity demanded decreases from q_0 to q_1 as the price decreases from p_0 to p_1. Prices p_0 and p_1 correspond to lines L_0 and L_1 in figure 6(a).

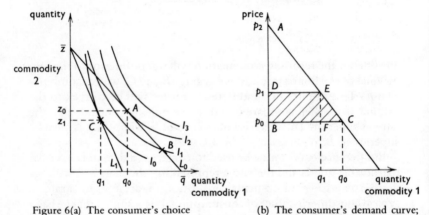

Figure 6(a) The consumer's choice

(b) The consumer's demand curve; consumer surplus

The demand curve can also be used to study the consumer's welfare loss stemming from a price increase. At price p_0, the last unit of the commodity that our individual consumes is worth exactly p_0 to him; when the price increases to p_1, he will decrease the quantity of the commodity that he demands until the last unit he consumes is worth exactly p_1 to him. Thus, in theory, every point on the demand curve indicates how much the consumer is willing to pay for an additional unit of the commodity. Note that if the price exceeds p_2 his demand for the commodity vanishes.

We are now in a position to define 'consumer surplus' as the sum of the difference between the maximal price the consumer is willing to pay to obtain one more unit of some commodity and the actual price he pays, p_0. The consumer surplus is rather large for the first unit consumed, $p_2 - p_0$; and it decreases for each successive unit consumed. For the last unit, the consumer surplus is zero. Thus, with a price of p_0, the consumer surplus for the amount q_0 is the triangle ABC. Likewise, when the price is p_1, the consumer surplus is given by the triangle ADE. The welfare loss due to the price increase is the difference between these two areas – the shaded area in figure 6(b). This decrease in consumer surplus can also be thought of as consisting of two parts: the increase in expenditure necessary to purchase q_1 units of the commodity at price p_1 rather than at price p_0, and the consumer surplus lost on those units which are no longer consumed. The former is represented by the rectangle $DEFB$ with an area of $(p_1-p_0)\,q_1$ while the latter is illustrated by the triangle ECF.

A similar line of reasoning can be used when one of the commodities is an environmental factor. Figure 7(a) presents an individual's indifference map for a marketable commodity and an environmental factor. The initial situation is characterized by the individual consuming z_0 units of the commodity, and q_0 units of the environmental factor, a consumption which yields the individual a welfare level of I_3 (point A in figure 7(a)). If the environment deteriorates so that the consumer can only obtain q_1 units of the environmental factor, the individual is forced to accept a lower welfare level, point B on I_2. If he is to retain his original utility, he must be able to buy $z_1-z_0 = BC$ more units of the market good. If environmental quality deteriorates even further, for example to point q_2, an even greater quantity of the market good is required for consumption, namely an increase of z_2-z_1 units.

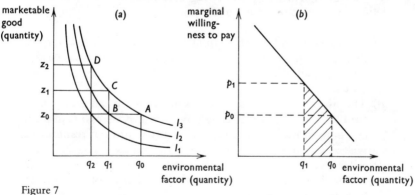

Figure 7
(a) Preferences and compensation

(b) The marginal
willingness to
pay; consumer
surplus

We can now derive a curve representing the consumer's marginal willingness to pay (MWP); the similarity to the demand curve should be obvious. This curve shows the quantity of a market good that an individual is willing to forgo to obtain an additional unit of the environmental factor, incomes being held constant. Conversely, the curve indicates the reward that an individual requires in order to accept a further deterioration of the environment. Thus, if the given quantity of the environmental factor is q_1, the individual requires compensation p_1 in order to accept a further decline in environmental quality by one unit. The indifference curves in figure 7(a) imply that the corresponding MWP curve has a negative slope. We can use the MWP curve to derive an individual welfare loss or gain for a given change in environmental quality. Note, however, if the environmental quality changes from q_1 to q_0, that the welfare gain is given by the *entire* shaded area as the individual does not pay for the environment and as the quantity of the environmental factor is given.

2.3 The perfect market economy

2.3.1 The main assumptions. We shall now use the concepts developed above to describe the perfect or pure market economy. This will include producers as well as consumers. Each such producer is characterized by a production possibility frontier, which states the possible alternative productions with a given level of technology. Further, the following assumptions are necessary to define the perfect market economy.

(a) The market is all encompassing – that is, all goods and services that affect the consumers' welfare are exchanged on the market. Similarly, all products and factors of production are exchanged on the market.
(b) The ownership of all natural resources and of all profits from firms is specified. In an economy with private ownership this assumption implies that the initial distribution of resources as well as the distribution of profits is completely specified.
(c) All transactions take place without cost – that is, no resources are required for transactions nor for the distribution of the information necessary for such transactions. Further, ownership is determined without cost.

Basic to a market economy is the existence of a price system in which there is a price for every commodity, and where this price is the same for both producers and consumers. That the market be all encompassing implies that every good and service has a price, which can be zero. These prices are at any given moment independent of the consumption and production programs of the economic agents; thus one speaks of prices as parameters. These given prices imply that each consumer has a given budget, dependent upon the distribution of the natural resources and on the profits of the firms. Within the framework of this budget, the individual chooses that pattern of consumption which yields him the highest welfare according to his own preferences.

Each production program implies costs for factors employed and income for products sold. Those production programs which require costs in excess of income are not feasible; the firm is assumed to choose that program which maximizes the difference between income and costs. In other words, the firm strives to obtain maximal profit.

2.3.2 Basic characteristics. A pure market economy has the following characteristics:

(a) Given preferences, technology, and ownership patterns, there exists a (unique) price system such that supply and demand are equated, for each good with a positive price, and if at all positive prices the supply exceeds the demand for any commodity, then that good's price is zero. This type of equilibrium is called a *competitive equilibrium*.

(b) In a competitive equilibrium, it is not possible to increase the production of one commodity without reducing the production of some other commodity. Thus, *production is efficient* in a competitive equilibrium.

(c) In a competitive equilibrium, it is not possible to increase the welfare of one consumer without reducing that of another. Thus *consumption is efficient* in a competitive equilibrium. Alternatively, we can state that a competitive equilibrium is *Pareto efficient*.

The theory says nothing about the final prices nor the final distribution of resources. In a market economy these are mainly dependent upon the initial distribution of resources and shares in the firms; while in a socialist economy, prices and distribution are dependent upon the norms dictated by the state. Equilibrium, efficiency in production, and Pareto efficiency do not preclude an extremely uneven distribution of welfare.[4] There is, however, a corollary to the theorem that allows us to retain certain basic elements of the market even after a rather far reaching redistribution of resources and ownership rights.

(d) Every Pareto efficient solution within an economy can be obtained by a suitable *redistribution* of ownership rights, initial endowments, and producers' profits.

Why are we interested in these abstract characteristics and how are they relevant to our long run planning? We shall shortly answer these questions; but first we will present an example that illustrates the above discussion in a simple economy.

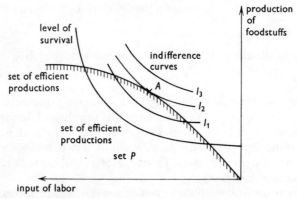

Figure 8 The individual's optimization without prices.

In figure 8 a very simplified economy with only one consumer is represented. He uses his own labor to produce a uniform produce here called foodstuffs. The model can easily be expanded to include any number of goods and consumers, but as we prefer to use simple diagrams rather than mathematics, this case will serve to illustrate the above arguments. Set *P* is the set of possible production programs and it represents as well the economy's technological possibilities. An efficient production implies that the individual as a producer chooses a program lying on the boundary of this set; from any point in the interior of *P* the producer can increase production

[4] We assume that the initial distribution allows all agents to survive. This is, however, not at all self evident, as underdeveloped countries aptly demonstrate.

without increasing the input of labor. The individual's preferences as a consumer are described by a system of indifference curves: these represent the economy's evaluation of each consumption program. Curve I_1 represents a lower welfare level than I_2, etc. An optimal program for work and consumption obtains at point A: it is impossible to find a feasible production program that gives higher welfare.

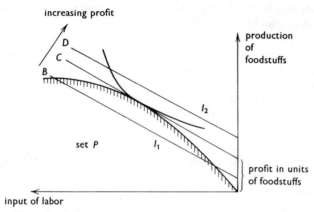

Figure 9 The individual maximizing his utility as a consumer and his profit as a producer with given system of prices.

The same solution to the allocation problem obtains if we assume a given set of prices at the same time as we give two roles to the individual, that of a producer and that of a consumer. The consumer would then sell his labor services at a fixed wage rate and purchase foodstuffs at a given price. The producer, conversely, would buy labor services and sell foodstuffs at the *same*, given prices. There is one wage and one price for the foodstuffs that yields equilibrium – or, rather more correctly, one relative price that results in equilibrium. Not only are demand and supply equal, but also an *optimum* allocation obtains. This equilibrium price corresponds to the slope of the line that separates the production possibility set from the indifference curve that gives the highest attainable preference levels (line *C* in figure 9).

This price system thus serves to 'separate'consumption and production decisions. If, given the optimal price, the producer maximizes his profits, then the amount produced will be equal to the amount the consumer would demand if he maximized his utility given the optimal price and an income equal to the sum of the profit he would have received if he owned the producing unit and the wages from sale of his labor services. This separation implies that the optimal production will obtain if the consumer maximizes his utility within the framework of his budget at the same time as the producer maximizes his profits given his production possibility set. The consumer's budget restriction – line C in figure 9 – is composed of his income from his labor as well as his share of profits in the firm; this budget, in turn, will be equal to the amount he spends on foodstuffs. Lines B, C, and D also represent differing profit levels for the firm at differing productions; given prices, all production programs on the same line yield the same profit. Line C represents the largest possible profit given the current technology embodied in the production possibility set.

The above characteristics can be extended to include an arbitrary number of consumers, producers, and commodities. In equilibrium it would not be possible for one consumer to increase his welfare without decreasing that of some other consumer; nor could any producer, by choosing another production program, increase his profits. Each producer will choose that production in which his marginal costs are exactly equal to the price of the good he produces. Further, equilibrium will prevail in all markets. There is nothing in the theory that prohibits us from considering equilibrium in any arbitrary number of future periods: we must, however, date all goods and services so that physically identical commodities produced in different time periods are considered as different goods.

2.3.3 The formation of prices. We shall now turn our attention to the process through which equilibrium may be reached: we shall suggest how a solution with the above outlined *optimum* and *equilibrium* properties can obtain through *decentralized* consumption and production decision making. We have only characterized the equilibrium solution: given the equilibrium prices, we have shown that if each consumer maximizes his utility and each producer maximizes his profits, then equilibrium results. However, to gain full insight into the advantages of decentralization and the information required for a market to function, we must study the process by which these equilibrium prices are established.

The planning process described here may be called the 'trial-and-error' planning method. The 'trial-and-error' part of the process is clearly seen below – successive trials are used and errors corrected as we approach the final, Pareto efficient solution. In the first stage in this process, a central planning agency (CPA) sets preliminary prices

– both current and future – for all goods and services. Each economic agent uses these prices to specify a preliminary production and/or consumption program, which he, in turn, presents to the CPA. This agency then simply sums all plans that it receives, compares the total supply with the total demand, and calculates new prices, which are then sent out to the economic agents. These new prices are set in such a way that, compared with the prices in the previous stage, they are increased for those goods where demand is greater than supply, and decreased for those where supply exceeds demand. The agents now suggest a new plan, and the CPA, in turn, calculates another set of prices; this process continues until demand and supply is equal for all goods and services. Note that if there is excess supply for a good in spite of a price equal to zero, this good will be a free good in equilibrium.

Figure 10 shows how decentralized decision making can lead to a

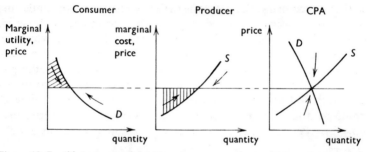

Figure 10 Equilibrium price formation

socially optimal solution. The diagram on the left represents the consumers. The curve labelled *D* shows how a consumer's marginal utility – normalized so that the curve represents the consumer's marginal rate of substitution between the commodity in question and some 'numeraire' – decreases with increasing consumption of the good. At a given price, the consumer considers if an increase in his consumption of a good yields higher welfare. A simple rule for him to follow is that if the price of the good is less that its marginal utility, then he should increase his consumption of that commodity; conversely, he should decrease consumption of it if its price exceeds its marginal utility. The consumer thus can approach his optimal situation through successive, marginal changes. The arrows in the diagram indicate the direction of change.

The center diagram presents a firm's marginal costs for producing the commodity. It can successively approach the optimum by increasing production if price is less than marginal costs, and by decreasing production when price is greater than marginal cost. Note that both consumer surplus and producer surplus obtain their respective maxima in that point where the consumer's marginal utility is equal to the producer's marginal cost; and both these are equal to the commodity's price.

The final diagram in figure 10 presents the CPA's part in equilibrium price formation: the agency changes prices depending on whether excess demand or supply characterizes the market. The arrows indicate the direction of the price adjustments.

We have here described an iterative process that takes place *before* any production or consumption occurs. However, this process, with certain modifications, can also be applied to the successive price adjustments in a market. We have indicated how the price system is crucial to the adjustment process: the only central decision made in this idealized market economy is the adjustment of prices according to the information contained in the summation of the actions of the various economic agents. Decentralization is also based on a rather simple behavioral rule: the maximization of individual welfare or business profits. Private efficiency, in equilibrium, corresponds to social efficiency. And with a given ownership pattern, initial distribution and technology, consumer preferences alone will determine the final production and its distribution.

2.4 The environment as a public good

The above analysis has assumed that the environmental factors were unaffected by production or consumption. We shall here change our approach and ask whether or not the environmental quality can be treated as a public good. A pure public good is a good whose consumption by one individual does not reduce the amount of it available for other consumers. In many cases, the above description is an apt description of an environmental factor: these often lie completely outside of the price system. The accepted theory for public goods has been developed by the Swedish economists Knut Wicksell and Erik Lindahl as well as by the American Paul Samuelson, although this theory was not primarily developed for environmental applications. Among other things, these economists have shown that an optimal quantity of a public good will not be produced in a decentralized market economy. If a consumer in such an economy wished to consume clean air, then he alone would have to bear the costs of producing it. However, all the other members of the economy would then receive an increase in their welfare without having to pay for it. As all consumers would prefer to be 'free riders', some basis for decision making other than that of the decentralized free market must be found if optimal production is to be obtained. Before we discuss alternative organizational forms that may be able to cope with the problem, we will sketch the welfare-theoretic solution where a Pareto efficient situation obtains, given both a public and a private good. A private good differs from a public good in that consumption of a private good by one individual prohibits another individual from consuming it (two people cannot eat the same orange!).

2.4.1 The optimal allocation between public and private goods. The diagram overleaf can be used to derive the optimal allocation of two goods – one private and the other public – between two individuals. Obviously, we can extend the analysis to include many goods and many individuals, but at the expense of a simple geometrical presentation.

In figure 11, (*a*) presents a set of indifference curves for individual *A*. These curves state his preferences for different combinations of the private and the public good. It should be noted that he is interested in his consumption of the public good, not that of other individuals in society. As usual, the individual is indifferent between consumption combinations which lie on the same curve; A_3 represents combinations preferred to A_2 and A_1; and so forth.

Figure (*b*) is the corresponding preference map for individual *B*. Note that we cannot state if a certain utility level for *A* is greater or less than a certain utility level for *B* without some sort of grounds for comparison.

Figure (*c*) depicts the set of socially efficient production combinations of the private and the public good. A solution must be a point on the curve *PP* if it is to be efficient.

We shall now solve for one of the infinitely many Pareto efficient solutions. To do so, we assign *B* an arbitrary utility level, B_2. The problem is now one of maximizing *A*'s welfare, given society's technological know-how, and *B*'s assigned welfare level. In order to solve this problem, we draw B_2 in diagram (*c*). Here the shaded area represents possible combinations of the public and the private good that satisfy the restriction in *B*'s welfare. As both individuals consume the entire production volume of the public good, the set of possible consumptions for *A* is found by subtracting B_2 from *PP* for

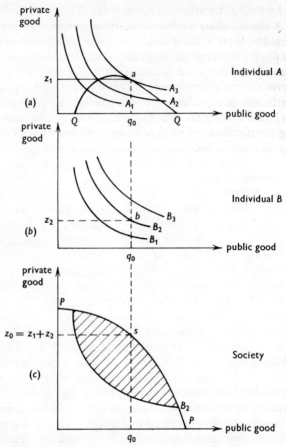

Figure 11   The optimal allocation of a private and a public good.

every possible production volume of the public good: that is, by considering the amount of the private good available for A's consumption given B's welfare level and the production of the public good. This vertical difference between PP and B_2 is drawn in diagram (a) as curve QQ. The highest obtainable utility level for A is represented by curve A_3 which is tangent to QQ in (a). This point represents a consumption of z_1 units of the private good and q_0 units of the public good.

Individual B, if he is to obtain utility level B_1 when q_0 units of the public good are produced, must consume z_2 units of the private one – that is, point b in the diagram. Note that this solution could also be derived by fixing A's utility at A_3 and maximizing B's utility as we did for A above. If we accept the resulting distribution of welfare represented by level A_3 for A and B_2 for B, the social equilibrium will be at the point s with a production and consumption of q_0 units of the public good, and $z_0=z_1+z_2$ units of the private one.

We wish to emphasize that the above solution is but one of many Pareto efficient ones; others obtain by assigning differing welfare levels to B and solving for the optimum. These solutions also imply differing distributions of welfare among the individuals as well as differing allocations between public and the private goods.

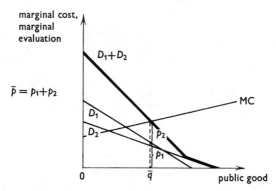

Figure 12 The optimal pricing of a public good.

Alternatively, we can use demand and supply curves to derive theoretically the optimal price and quantity of an environmental factor. This method is illustrated in figure 12. It is here assumed that the environmental factor studied is 'small' in comparison to the economy at large – that is, the analysis is one of partial rather than general equilibrium. Each individual is assumed to have a demand curve which indicates the greatest amount he is willing to pay in order to obtain an extra unit of the environmental factor. It is reasonable to assume that these demand curves, or marginal willing-ness to pay (MWP) curves, have a negative slope: the individual is willing to pay a rather large sum for the first unit, and less and less for each succeeding one. In figure 12 we have drawn two such curves, D_1 and D_2, representing two individuals.

We have said that a pure public good is consumed in its entirety by each individual in society. Thus when we seek the optimal output of such a good, we should sum over all individuals willing to pay for an additional unit. This total willingness to pay should then be compared with the cost of producing an additional unit. That is, we sum all individuals' MWP curves *vertically* and compare the resulting curve with society's marginal costs.

The optimal production in figure 12 is $\bar{q}$. To the left of this point, consumers are willing to pay more than it costs to produce an additional unit; to the right of $\bar{q}$ costs exceed willingness to pay. The optimal prices are p_1 for individual 1, and p_2 for individual 2; note that the optimal total price is $\bar{p}=p_1+p_2$. If these are set via taxes, all costs are covered and the optimum obtains (with marginal costs increasing as in figure 12 we even get a profit!). Such 'pseudo-prices' for each individual – a price that is determined by his MWP – will lead to an equilibrium of sorts.

Other methods for financing the production of public goods exist, and the method with 'pseudo-prices' is mainly of theoretical interest. If the initial solution is one with no production of the public good, then an optimum solution that is also Pareto efficient obtains if the consumers are charged prices p_1 and p_2. This implies that a movement from 0 to $\bar{q}$, with the above mentioned prices, will decrease no one's welfare and lead to a clear welfare gain for at least one individual.

One of the implications of the existence of public goods is that the competitive equilibrium will not necessarily generate solutions with efficient consumption: the production of public goods will be less than the optimal quantity, while that of private goods, for which functioning markets already exist will be greater than the optimum. Indeed, many public goods will not even be produced in a pure market economy. If efficient consumption is to obtain, other methods of allocation must be sought; the market must be complemented with some type of organization capable of determining the amount of public goods to be produced.

While the theoretical models described above give a general description of solutions yielding efficient consumption, they are of rather little help to the politician wishing to implement such a program. Possibly the model would serve as a guideline for a benevolent dictator with an ample supply of truth serum and a gigantic computer – the former to entice his subjects to reveal their true preferences, the latter to calculate the optimal solution. The problem of finding the socially correct production levels of both public and private goods is an issue for democratic social planners as well as for command economies. As we shall see, democratic planners must offer concrete programs which allow consumers' preferences to determine the optimal production levels, and must not dismiss the problem with meaningless generalizations such as how society must 'use democratic methods to plan for the future'.

A possible way out of this dilemma is to let the government conduct consumer surveys in order to gain insight into consumer preferences. However, such surveys are rather difficult to implement. If one attempts to estimate individuals' MWP curves $-D_1$ and D_2 in figure 12 – but cannot couple the stated willingness to pay with the actual fee paid, individuals will tend to overstate their preferences and the result will be a greater than optimal production of public goods.

If, on the other hand, one does couple the individual's stated preferences to the fee he pays for the public good, he will have a strong incentive to understate his true valuations: as the public good is available for all, each individual will rather let others pay while he gets a 'free ride'. For in a large society, a single person's payments are small in comparison to the total sum collected. This problem is often described as a $1/N$ problem: given a society with N individuals, one individual's willingness to pay is but $1/N$ of the total willingness to pay.

During recent years, economists have constructed a number of laboratory experiments, on the basis of modern game and statistical theories, and so designed that the individuals are motivated to state their correct preferences. However, the step between such abstract experiments and political reality is still a large one, even if the results do seem promising.

That the practical solution to the above problem will be some form of voting was recognized by Wicksell. Such voting procedures would serve as a channel of communication between individuals and decision makers. However, such voting procedures are rather expensive and often theoretically inadequate as the example in section 2.1.1 aptly demonstrates.

Even if voting procedures much more sophisticated than those used in practical situations were employed there is no guarantee that such procedures would produce situations with the optimal characteristics described above. That is to say, such procedures will not necessarily result in production levels where the sum of the individuals' MWPs is equal to the social marginal cost.

As voting procedures that include all members of society are extremely expensive to implement, some cheaper method must be found. In democratic societies, these costs have led to the development of representative democracy, often with but a few political parties and regionally scheduled elections. While this solution has to do with political life in general, its parallel to a decentralized market economy is obvious. Indeed, an area for further research would be to see which forms of representative democracy give results which approach the optimal allocations described in theoretical models. In all probability, we would find political imperfections akin to the much better known market imperfections. This difference can partially be explained by the fact that political theory is much less developed than economic theory. To study problems in political science from the angle suggested here – how to guide economic allocation and distribution in cases where either no market exists or the existing market functions poorly – might seem rather strange to political scientists. Above all, this approach involves normative comparisons between actual and theoretical processes.

2.5 The theory of externalities in environmental policy

We are now in a position to combine the two different theoretical approaches outlined above. The households' welfare is a function both of goods consumed and the environmental quality in which they live. On the commodity market, the individual will choose that consumption which maximizes his welfare, given commodity prices and his income. However, he cannot adjust his consumption of environmental services in the same manner: he must accept the environmental quality as it is. Because of the collective nature of the environment, an individual cannot – indeed, as we have seen, he has little incentive to even attempt to – improve its quality.

The firms in turn choose the production program that maximizes their individual profits. However, during the production processes wastes are produced and released into the environment – wastes that to a greater or lesser degree affect the environment. The social cost of these discharges depends on the households' evaluation of the environment, a value dependent on the households' marginal willingness to pay. The problem is, however, that the size of the MWP is not revealed on any market.

The theoretical solution to many environmental policy problems can be presented in a simple diagram (figure 13). The upper part of this diagram depicts a market for a private commodity – it contains the demand curve and the firms' direct marginal costs as well as the social marginal cost curve which is the sum of private marginal costs and the MWP curve.

The usual equilibrium, A, obtains where the firms' marginal private costs are equal to the price that equates demand and supply.

The lower half of the diagram illustrates how the marginal willingness to pay increases with a decreasing environmental quality. We assume that the degree of pollution is directly proportional to the production volume, and we measure the *MWP* downwards on the y-axis.

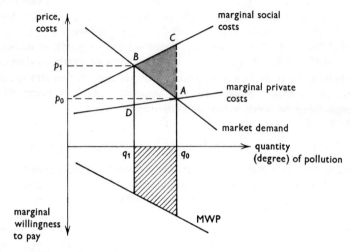

Figure 13 Externalities and environmental policy.

Let us imagine a rather sophisticated environmental protection agency (EPA) that knows the exact form of the consumers *MWP* curves and has the power to force firms to fully compensate consumers for worsened environmental quality. Obviously A is no longer the equilibrium solution. If the production decreases from q_0 to q_1, consumers are willing to pay an amount corresponding to the corresponding movement along the *MWP* curve. Such a decrease in production leads to a decrease in the combined producer and consumer surplus by the amount in triangle ABD. However, as pollution decreases as production decreases, the consumer surplus increases by the amount of the shaded area under the *MWP* curve. Because of the way the marginal social cost curve is constructed, this shaded area is equal to the area $ACBD$. So the end result of the production decrease is a social gain corresponding to triangle CBA.

The social marginal cost curve can be given two different interpretations. First, it shows the cost to the firm if it is made to bear the entire cost of its discharges into the environment. This cost is charged to the firm by the EPA and corresponds to the amount necessary to compensate the consumers for the pollution connected with the productive processes. In this way, the firm can be made to consider the marginal social cost instead of the marginal private cost in its production plans. If the EPA cannot enforce such a compensatory policy, the difference between this curve and the marginal private cost curve indicates the potential compensation needed to reimburse the households for the worsened environmental quality resulting from an increase in commodity production.

A decrease in production from q_0 to q_1, and the resulting price increase from p_0 to p_1 results in a socially optimal combination of commodity production and environmental quality, as long as one does not consider the possibility that a different production method would result in less pollution. A further decrease in production past q_1 is not optimal as the MWP – or, rather, the marginal compensatory claim – for a further decrease in pollution would be less than the resultant decrease in the combined producer and consumer surplus.

Note that if the existing production of the commodity is q_0, it may be profitable for the consumers to organize themselves and offer to pay the firm to reduce production. Obviously there are a number of different solutions, depending upon who compensates whom, representing different distributions of the resulting gain when production is changed from the suboptimal q_0 to the optimal q_1.

A similar diagram can be used to demonstrate some of the aspects of an *active* environmental policy. Figure 14 presents essentially the same problem as we studied in figure 13 but with the possibility of purifying plant wastes explicitly considered. Thus the main difference between the two figures is the inclusion of a cost function for waste processing included in figure 14.

This cost function, drawn in the lower half of the diagram, shows how environmental quality can be improved at a constant cost per unit of waste processed. Given the cost for waste processing in figure 14, consumers experience a welfare gain if the wastes are processed so that the level of pollution is reduced to q_2; but note that further improvement would involve costs that exceed MWP. If the EPA elects to allow the firm to choose between compensation or processing, the firm will face a new marginal cost curve – one that is discontinuous at point G. For a production volume lower than G (i.e. lower than q_2) compensation is cheaper; for a production volume greater than G, it is cheaper to process wastes, thus improving environmental quality. Once a waste processing plant is built, the firm will choose to produce q_3 units of the commodity. That is, F will be the new optimum on the commodity market and q_2 will be the optimal environmental quality. Thus we have, via processing, obtained both a better environment $(q_2<q_1)$ and a larger commodity output $(q_3>q_1)$.

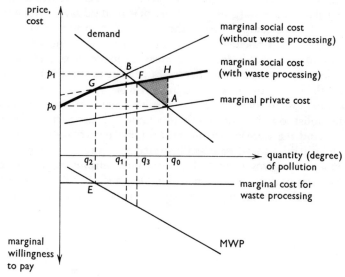

Figure 14 Externalities and environmental policy (with waste processing).

The diagram can also be used to present a non-optimal policy. Assume that the firm has no financial responsibility for the pollution its methods cause, that is, we are at point A with production q_0. Given the degree of pollution associated with this production volume, the consumers can obtain greater welfare by building a processing plant, and thereby obtaining an environmental quality corresponding to q_2. However, this separation of production and waste disposal decisions leads to a definite loss to society, a loss given by triangle HFA. This loss exists as the production of q_0-q_3 units of the commodity are sold at p_0, a price too low as the real costs for processing this production volume are greater than the increase in consumer surplus that these units produce.

2.6 Monopoly and externalities

In the previous section we demonstrated how society could gain (eliminate a welfare loss) by reducing production (see figure 13). This claim is not always valid if only *one* firm produces the commodity in question. To see why this is so, study figure 15. A monopolist produces until his marginal cost and marginal revenue are equal. In figure 15, z is the difference between the price and the marginal revenue at the untaxed level of production q_0. Note that the difference between the marginal social and marginal private cost is d, less than z. If we attempt to force the monopolist to use the marginal social cost in his calculations, we could do so by setting a tax a per unit of production. He will then decrease production to q_1. However, this decrease in production decreases consumer surplus by q_1ABq_0 while the social cost for this production is but q_1DCq_0. We conclude that a net loss to society, $ABCD$, results when we force a polluting monopolist to reduce production by taxing his production. On the other hand, if z were less than d at the original level of production, we would obtain a social gain as illustrated in figure 16. The decrease from q_2 to q_1 gives a decrease in consumer surplus of q_1ABq_2; the social costs of this production are q_1CDq_2. If CAE is less than BDE, society gains in welfare by levying a unit tax of a on the firm.

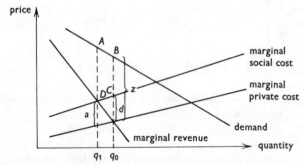

Figure 15 A tax on monopoly production which results in a welfare loss.

We conclude that if we try to correct for one deficiency – pollution – in a market where there exists another deficiency – monopoly – the result may well be a further welfare loss.

2.7 Summary and conclusions

This chapter deals mainly with basic welfare economics and gives the theoretical background for analyzing environmental problems as market imperfections. The chapter carefully explains the meaning of social efficiency calculations and stresses the difference between social and private costs and benefits in economic analysis especially

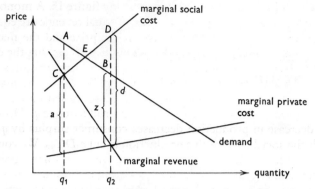

Figure 16 A tax on monopoly production which results in a welfare gain.

with regard to environmental problems. In order to make these distinctions it is also necessary to discuss the theoretical basis for measuring individual welfare measurements. Given this information the chapter goes on to state the assumptions and basic characteristics of a pure market economy. The main conclusion from this is that when the market fails to encompass some commodities which affect the consumers' welfare no optimal allocation of resources can be achieved by means of uncontrolled market behavior. Because this is a characteristic feature of a working economy, there is need for further examination of these phenomena. This is done in the rest of the chapter by showing how the environment can be regarded as a public good and how the theory of externalities can be used in designing environmental policy. The existence of market imperfections explains the need for a public policy with respect to the allocation of scarce environmental resources. This policy must however always take into account the conditions in the rest of the economy. To illustrate some of these problems the chapter ends with a short note on 'second best' problems in formulating an optimal environmental policy.

3
An economic analysis of environmental policy

The preceding chapter demonstrated that many environmental policy problems can be thought of as instances where the price system does not convey sufficient information for the market to function properly. Various corrective measures must be applied to the market if it is to function satisfactorily. However, abstract theory is one thing, and the practical application of it another. This chapter will attempt to bridge the gap between theory and practice by considering a number of concrete environmental policy problems. We shall emphasize the economic nature of these problems and suggest how the various corrective measures can best be applied.

We consider first the problem of environmental quality and recreational activity. This is a problem that lies close to that of public goods: how does one best set a price on nature as a recreational facility? If such a price can be found, many decisions, such as the choice between industrial exploitation or the retention of 'untouched' nature, or the restoration of despoiled areas, are made easier.

The second example is the problem presented by litter: this problem is central to the choice between returnable and non-returnable bottles. It appears that no simple solutions are obtainable as one must balance the costs connected with the collection and shipments of the returned bottles against the welfare loss caused by discarded bottles.

The third and fourth examples are two classical 'emissions problems': the emission of phosphates (mainly from detergents) into lakes and rivers and the emission of sulphur dioxide into the atmosphere (with the destruction of farmland as one of the final effects). As both water and air are difficult to incorporate into the price system, the main concern is where in the production chain control measures should be taken: at the source of the pollution (the phosphates in the detergents or the sulphur in the oil) or at the places where the actual emission occurs. These two problems also allow a discussion of effluent charges or emission standards as the main instrument in environmental protection.

The fifth example is similar to the two preceding ones: that of lead in gasoline. Once again, one can weigh the advantages and disadvantages of both taxation and regulation. However, as lead accumulates in both animal and plant tissue, there is here a further complication: that of contaminated products being sold to consumers.

The final example considers the type of environment one encounters in factories. This example is intended to show that different types of environmental discussions (the natural environment, the home environment, the factory environment) have very little besides the word 'environment' in common. Correspondingly, the corrective measures that need to be applied in each case are substantially different.

3.1 Environmental quality and recreational activities

In chapter two we explained why certain environmental factors lie outside the price system and thus cannot be bought or sold on the market. In order to set a price on the use of an environmental factor such as flowing water (with its self-cleansing ability), one must obtain some estimate of the damage or costs to other water users that stem from a certain user's activity.

The classical example of a negative externality is a firm dumping an organic waste into a river, thus reducing the production possibilities of other firms as well as the recreational quality of the river for bathing and sports fishing. Thus, in estimating the extent of the damage caused, we must consider the increased cost to other water using firms and the forgone recreational opportunities. The size of the first of these two items is rather easy to specify; the second is much more difficult, though not impossible, to estimate empirically. We emphasize that it is extremely important that this last item be included in the calculations as many decisions in environmental care directly affect the recreational value of nature.

3.1.1 The Delaware study: certain conclusions. One of the more comprehensive studies of a water quality improvement project was undertaken in connection with the measures planned for the Delaware River in the United States. This study gives invaluable data with which to investigate the possibilities of introducing a system of effluent charges to improve water quality to comply with stated

standards. The project was planned for a stretch of the Delaware that had a long history of pollution by oxygen demanding organic wastes, which had led to recurrent destruction of fish life in that sector of the river.

The relationship between the various discharges and water quality was studied using a mathematical model constructed to include both the chemical and biological aspects of the problem. The model, based on a division of the river into thirty different sectors, made it possible to study the effect of an emission in one sector on the water quality in another. As the model was a linear one, linear programming methods were used to determine the minimum cost for obtaining differing water qualities. The procedure was repeated using more and more stringent standards in order to study both total costs and the costs associated with a given improvement in water quality. The actual standard to be implemented depended on the advantages from the improved water quality accruing to the industrial, municipal, and recreational users of the river. However, the gains to the first two above named users were insignificant compared to those accruing to the recreational users. Certain industries actually displayed increased costs, as the increased oxygen content of the water led to an increase in corrosion in their machines.

The largest increase in welfare accrued undoubtedly to the recreational users: those who used the river for fishing, boating, and bathing. This in turn implies that there did exist a demand for recreational opportunities that was dependent upon water quality. It was then possible to construct a curve showing the aggregated marginal willingness to pay for water quality, the theoretical basis of which was presented in chapter two. Figure 17 shows how such a

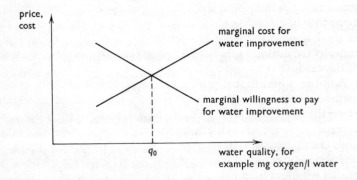

Figure 17 The determination of optimal water quality.

curve might appear, as well as the marginal cost curve for water improvement. The intersection between these two curves indicates the optimal water quality.

The Delaware study highlights the importance of recreational uses in determining optimal water quality. However, the services provided by recreational activity are rather different from those produced by traditional goods and services. Because of the common belief that these services cannot be assigned a money value, investment projects tend to use but rough estimates in assigning a value to these services. However, modern welfare theory, with its analysis of externalities and public goods, affords us the chance of assigning these services a more exact value. Almost no commodity has an infinite or a zero value; individuals or groups usually have some notion as to how many units of a certain commodity they are willing to offer in order to obtain additional recreational possibilities. This should not be taken to imply that such activities should be commercially exploited: we are not advocating that they be sold on a market. These economic values can be an important guidepost for future planners even if they do not directly increase the GDP.

Recent economic research into this field has developed various methods of estimating recreational value. These may be divided into two main categories:

(1) Methods based on an indirect estimation of the willingness to pay; and
(2) Methods based on direct estimation of willingness to pay.

Both methods aim at establishing a demand curve for outdoor recreational activity. The first group of methods are usually theoretically weaker than the second group, but are usually easier to apply in actual cases. An example is the use of the market price of fish and game to assign a 'value' to the activities of fishing and hunting. This method, however, grossly underestimates these values as it does not consider the intrinsic value of the activity itself, regardless of the size of the catch.

A more sophisticated and theoretically more correct indirect method is based upon the actual behavior of recreational consumers, especially the amount they are willing to pay for trips and other expenses incurred in connection with such activity. These observations can then be used to construct a demand curve. In contrast, the direct method is based on interviews which then provide an estimate of this willingness to pay.

3.1.2 Preferences and consumer behavior. This section presents a closer examination of methods for estimating recreational values. To begin with, one must distinguish between the demand for the entire recreational process or experience, and the demand for the relevant recreational resource in itself. The process encompasses five different phases: (1) planning; (2) travel to the area; (3) the activities in the recreational area – recreation in the narrow sense; (4) travel from the area; and (5) the aftermath.[1] Using the demand for the entire process, one can derive the demand for the resource itself. The first problem is, then, to define the resource in terms of price and quantity variables using the three different types of recreational costs: money cost, time cost, and 'enjoyment' cost (in terms of an enjoyable or disagreeable experience).

To illustrate the calculation of demand curves, we will for the moment ignore all but the monetary costs. As these must be relevant to the entire recreational process, they must include travel expenses, room and board, the recurring costs for equipment, and, when relevant, entrance fees. These are the immediate costs. The relevant quantity variable should be the number of visits to the area, rather than the number of visitors, as the same person can visit the site a number of times during any period. This quantity variable should then be presented in terms of the number of visits per 1000 individuals (say) in the base population in order to remove the effect of the population distribution within the area under study. This sort of variable will be of the same type as per capita income or per capita consumption.

This line of reasoning can be illustrated in a diagram such as figure 18. For a given recreational area such as a mountain resort, we study the number of visits per 1000 individuals in populations that have differing monetary costs. Those individuals living in the proximity of the resort have a rather low cost per visit, and thus rather many visits per 1000 individuals; this group is represented by point *B*. On the other hand, those living far from the resort have a high cost per visit such as in point *E*. By combining all such points representing groups with differing monetary costs and visits per 1000 individuals, we can derive a demand curve for the recreational process.

The problem is now to assign the recreational resource a value, that is, to determine the social value of the resource. If we assume that the different groups have similar tastes and incomes, and if the

[1] M. Clawson, J. Knetsch, *Economics of Outdoor Recreation*, Baltimore 1966.

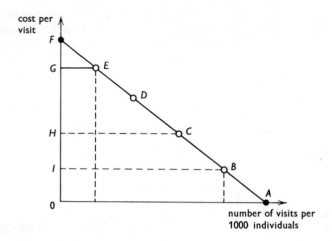

Figure 18 The demand for a recreational process.

differences in the frequencies of their visits are due largely to the differing costs, then the following holds.

If those visitors in group B were charged an entrance fee for each visit, say a fee equal to HI in figure 18, they would then exhibit the same frequency as group C has without the entrance fee. If one increases the fee so that group B has the same costs as group E, they both would visit the resort equally often.

The social value of a recreational resource can now be defined as the difference between the largest sum the individuals as a group would be willing to pay to utilize the resource less the actual cost for those resources used during their visit. Thus, for group B, the resource's value corresponds to the triangle BFI: the maximum amount that could be charged by discriminatory entrance fees. Likewise, EFG is the corresponding amount for group E. The total social value is then found by multiplying the average of the 'consumer surplus' of the respective groups by the number of individuals in the population.

Figure 19 shows the demand curve for the resource derived in this manner. The value of the resource corresponds to the area under the curve, that is, ABO. This sum is usually called the consumer surplus, and can also be thought of as the social value of the resource. An important assumption made here is that congestion is no problem: the presence of an additional visitor is assumed not to affect the other visitors' utilization of the resource. Note the difference between the

demand for the entire recreational *process* and that for the resource
itself: the demand for the latter is determined indirectly by studying
the behavior of individuals having differing costs for the former.

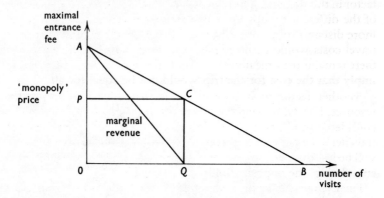

Figure 19 The demand for a recreational resource.

We can use figure 19 to demonstrate that charging an entrance fee
that does not correspond to the actual cost of using the resource will
lead to an sub-optimal use of society's resources. As, within reasonable limits, our mountain resorts do not show increasing depreciation as the number of visitors increases, the optimal price charged
should be zero. The demand curve shows how much a perfectly
discriminating monopolist would be able to charge: in theory, each
individual would pay a fee identical to the maximum amount he
would be willing to pay and still make the visit. If the resort is run by
a normal profit maximizing monopolist, he lacks this information.
He will then set a price so that his marginal costs are equal to his
marginal revenue: the price set will be P. The number of visitors
decreases from B to Q, and the firm obtains a profit of OP times OQ,
that is $OPCQ$; this profit does not accrue from any real production,
other than the rather unproductive sale of entrance tickets. Obviously, setting this price robs the consumers of part of their surplus.
Similarly, the price charged will result in a lowering of the number of
visits, from B to Q. As there are, by assumption, no real economic
costs connected with a visit, the price P leads to a welfare loss for
society; and this welfare loss can be approximated by the lost consumer surplus, QCB.

The purely monetary costs are not the only ones that determine
the demand for a recreational resource. We must also consider the

costs of the time spent on and the enjoyment gained from the visit, factors which are to some extent dependent on each other. The time required for the visit to the resource is undoubtedly an important factor in this demand. The recreational area's location relative to that of the different groups must be carefully determined. Even if the more distant groups could be reimbursed for the trip, so that their travel costs would be no higher than those living near the resort, there remains the time necessary for the journey. This in turn would imply that the cost for the trip would not be equal for all.

Another factor to be considered is the actual journey to the resource. If those making the trip find it dull and boring, this will be considered an additional cost of visiting the recreational area, and the traveller's demand for the area will be reduced – that is, his demand will be less than the monetary costs would indicate. If the journey is stimulating, the opposite holds.

Finally, one can criticize the indirect methods of assessing costs and benefits just because they are indirect. An increase in the cost of a visit can be thought of as an increase in entrance fees, or an increase in other costs that elicits a similar response from the persons involved. But will these persons really react to this cost increase as they would to others? We do not know to what extent they would have changed their consumption patterns in the absence of the cost increase: we lack information as to how elastic demand for one good is to price changes in other goods. Again, the indirect methods are unsatisfactory if the entire population lives close to the recreational area, and differing travel costs cannot readily be observed. Some individuals can value the resource highly even if they live close to it. Direct methods do, however, provide a means for resolving these issues.

The direct methods, as do the indirect ones, aim at determining the marginal willingness to pay using appropriately chosen questions. For example, one can ask what is the maximum one is prepared to pay for a certain recreational resource. But unless the answer is directly associated with the price to be paid, there is the risk that the individual will overstate his willingness, especially if he believes that a certain area may be closed or that improvements are being planned.

Within the framework of western democracies, the only practical solution is the political one. However, studies based on direct or indirect methods may play an important role in the decision process. This is especially true when it is necessary to choose between two or more potential users of the resource. An example is the widely discussed future for the rivers in the north of Sweden. In this debate the recreational value is recognized, but not considered measurable in monetary terms. Here a scientific study would have indicated the recreational value of the river. As there will always be such conflicts in connection with river development projects, the physical planning of the country should explicitly consider recreational value. The example of the Delaware study indicates the necessity of considering such aspects, as the greatest gains from water quality improvement fell to recreational users.

3.2 Returnable and non-returnable containers

During recent years, the advantages and disadvantages of different types of containers – especially for beer and soft drinks – have been intensely debated. It has been pointed out that the non-returnable bottles and cans widely used and often discarded in nature cause injuries to both wildlife and man as well as reducing the aesthetic value of nature. It has further been argued that these non-returnable containers adversely affect household waste disposal: an increased production of non-returnable containers will not only increase the total amount of waste, but will, given certain disposal methods, lead to an increase in by-products that damage the environment. For example, the burning of wastes containing PVC plastics will result in the pollution of the atmosphere with the accompanying risk of precipitation of acidic materials. The cost of incinerating the wastes also increases.

It is important to note that these beer and soft drink containers are but a small percentage of total household wastes. So the different proposals to deal with this problem only solve a small part of the larger problem of waste disposal.

3.2.1 The nature of the problem. The discussion of returnable versus non-returnable containers does, however, shed light on the problem of optimal waste disposal. *Non-returnable* bottles and tins can be discarded either in nature or along with the other household wastes. *Returnable* bottles, on the other hand, can also be recycled.

The discarding of a container of either type in nature implies that a certain piece of land is pre-empted by this container for a greater or shorter period of time. Ideally we would let the person who threw the bottle in nature bear the costs to society that this action implies. The tax imposed should be equal to the cost of removing it or the compensation to the other consumers necessary to remove the disutility caused by the littering. This tax should be placed on both non-returnable and returnable containers as the latter may also be

An economic analysis   51

discarded in nature. Further, a container thrown in an out-of-the-way place where few would come across it should be charged a lower tax than one thrown in a much frequented location. However, such a system of taxes is not feasible, as it implies that each and every container be assigned a unique tax dependent on its removal and compensation costs.

One way out of this dilemma is to place an equal charge on all containers (the *low-tax* method). The aim of this tax should be to compensate society for the problems caused by the discarding of containers in nature. The tax would be refunded on returnable containers when they were returned. However, such a tax (on both types of containers) must be calculated on average costs, that is the total environmental cost of discarded cans divided by the total number of cans produced. This does not solve the allocation problem as the tax would be rather low. So the refund on returnable containers would only increase a small amount, as would the price of non-returnable containers. Therefore the incentive to consume fewer non-returnable containers would be weak as the price difference between the two types would be small. A certain amount of justice would be achieved as those who used non-returnable containers would pay as a group for the damage they caused, but such justice is not the primary goal of environmental policy.

3.2.2 A legal approach. A solution to the allocation problem requires other methods. In what follows we shall discuss three alternative ways, based on the principle that he who litters must be made aware of the actual costs to society created by his action. The first method considered is aimed at creating this awareness but does not differentiate between returnable and non-returnable containers. This method is the *legal* one, and its basic premise is that it should be declared illegal to litter. Those caught littering will be charged a 'littering fee' or fine, the size of which will depend on

(1) society's evaluation of the unpleasantness of a littered environment – a welfare loss due to the cost of cleaning up the mess or the unpleasant sight of garbage in nature; and
(2) the probability of detection.

While it is difficult to specify precise values for these two items, they do represent a possible solution. Assume, for example, that the average inconvenience for litter is valued at one krona. Indeed it has been estimated that the cleaning costs alone are as high as 0.50 kronor/container. If we assume that the container will have lain in

nature some time before it is collected, then an average social cost of
1 krona is not unreasonable. If the probability of detection is 0.1 per
cent, then the fine should be 1000 kronor. Note that this method is
aimed only at those who discard empty containers in nature, and not
those who discard them along with other household trash. Even
though this method uses society's costs in calculating the fine, there
are disadvantages associated with it. As the probability of being
caught is much smaller than in the above example, an effective fine
must be very large indeed. The other side of the coin is, of course,
that such large fines are efficient deterrents. One can interpret the
fine as a *random* price charged for littering.

3.2.3 The high-tax method. Another, totally different approach to
the problem is to introduce a *high-tax* method, in contrast to the
low-tax one described above. If society's cost for a drink container
discarded in nature is 1 krona, then a system placing a tax equal to
this on every container gives the following solution. A fee of 1 krona
is levied on each container as it leaves the production process. For
returnable containers this fee will be paid back to the consumer when
he returns the container to the store; for non-returnable containers
the tax would be repaid when the container was delivered to special
processing or trash collection stations. A clear disadvantage with this
method is the increase in administrative effort needed, as it is no
longer 'economical' to throw non-returnable containers in the
household trash can. It should be pointed out that this type of tax
system can be successfully employed in other cases where the emission of wastes results in pollution, and where it is difficult to control
such emissions. Heavy metals used in limited quantities and capable
of being recycled via special processes (if they are not washed down
the drain) can, in principle, easily be included in such a system of
deposit taxes. Even the problem of used automobiles can be solved in
this manner.

   A more difficult problem with this method is that the deposit may
well be repaid for containers that have not initially paid the tax. If the
deposit is high enough, people will be motivated either to produce
containers or to import them in order to cash in on the deposit. The
method must thus be coupled with a number of administrative
controls in order to prevent such misuses.

3.2.4 Propaganda. A third and often employed method is that of
propaganda rather than direct economic incentives. While the two
previous methods are based on rewards – the deposit – or punish-

ments – the establishment of high fines for littering – the propaganda campaigns ('Keep Britain tidy') aim at changing attitudes and appeal directly for solidarity with society, even if it is much easier for the individual to discard the container where convenient rather than in a socially more acceptable place.

However, there are limits to the effectiveness of such campaigns. As the degree of solidarity with society is in all likelihood rather low, such campaigns should be aimed at areas where their effects are the greatest or administrative control the most difficult. Further, for campaigns and similar appeals to be effective they require a high degree of environmental awareness among the consumers: instead of using taxes, prices, deposits, or punishments which only influence people through their own self-interest, campaigns, to be effective, require that each consumer be his own environmental care agency.

3.2.5 Prohibition. The method which is claimed to be the most efficient means of eliminating the undesirable side effects of non-returnable containers is to forbid their production. This solution, however, can be criticized in a number of ways. First of all, forbidding the production of non-returnable bottles, for example, does not solve the environmental problems caused by returnable ones, although an increased deposit here would help matters. Secondly, the advantages of using non-returnable containers may outweigh the disadvantages. If this be the case, then prohibiting them will also eliminate the advantages they have; it would be better to use the methods outlined above. We should point out, however, that drink containers represent but a small part of the problem that littering poses: even if we could successfully divert all such containers from nature to more appropriate processing places, the problem of littering would remain. As our goal is to reduce littering, not the use of non-returnable bottles, we should take measures that will be effective against all littering. The relevant question seems to be how great an increase in resources is required to reduce problems accruing from drink containers to an acceptable level, given the current effort to reduce all littering. It is the answer to this question that should be compared with the other methods for eliminating littering. Note that measures aimed at eliminating the problem in its entirety can also be combined with a prohibition of non-returnable containers. However, only those containers whose 'litter effects' are greatly in excess of the average litter effect should be forbidden.

We suggest that this increase in costs is relatively small in the case where the new measures taken are directed towards reducing total littering, including drink containers. Such methods as an increase in information, in the number of trash cans, in propaganda campaigns, and in fines for littering will not remove the entire problem created by littering but this is not necessarily a social goal. It is efficient to increase measures against littering only as long as the total benefits exceed the total costs. Thus it is plain that society should aim at eliminating all littering, as the effort required to remove the last few percentage points may well exceed society's evaluation of the difference between a litter-free and an almost litter-free world.

3.2.6 The problem of trash. The above analysis was based on the assumption that the households faced a correct price for garbage collection, a price that also included the environmental costs of discarding wastes in the household trash can. That is, that the collection fees were assumed to express not only transportation and processing costs but also those costs such as air and water pollution resulting from the various processing methods. Indeed, even the aesthetic effects of garbage dumps should be included.

One is here confronted by two problems. Municipal trash collection and processing is based on average costs that include only the strictly monetary ones: the increased pollution or lost aesthetic values are not included. Thus one concludes that the amount of household wastes will be larger than the socially optimal amount. Secondly, as trash collection is often financed out of municipal taxes, a household that increases its amount of trash will not find its taxes increase in the same proportion: the increase in costs will be borne by all residents in the area. We have a classic 1/N problem. Both of these problems can be solved by including all costs in calculating collection fees, and by adjusting individual household fees in accordance with the amount – say weight and volume – of trash that each one produces. In this way a socially optimal amount of garbage will obtain.

3.3 Recycling

If society has declared its intention of reducing energy consumption, it has various methods at hand to obtain its goal. One of these which is already in use today is the recycling of certain containers, especially drink containers. The obvious advantage of recycling is that returnable containers can be used more than once while the economic value of a non-returnable container disappears when emptied.

One can affect the number of times that a given container is recycled by adjusting the deposit on it. An increase in this fee, directly or indirectly via a production tax, increases the economic incentive for returning the bottle and thereby receiving the deposit. Why not then produce only returnable containers and set a high deposit to increase their circulation? There are several good reasons why such a solution is not practical.

(A) For reasons of hygiene, certain types of containers are not suitable for recycling. Examples are milk cartons, anchovy tins, plastic bread wrappings, and so on.

(B) A method of collection points must be established. This work has progressed to some extent in the drinks industry, where machines that electronically scan bottles and determine the deposit due on them now exist. However, the problem remains for such containers as empty toothpaste tubes, empty flour bags, empty shoe boxes, etc.

There is no doubt that the problems must be mitigated if the goal of a decrease in the amount of refuse is to be attained. The chief aim is to recycle all the raw materials in household wastes. Today attempts are being made to realize this aim: in some places the households themselves sort the refuse into broad categories like paper, plastics, glass, etc. These materials are then used as raw materials in different industries.

3.3.1 Recycling and transaction costs. Before recycling is possible, there must be buyers willing to purchase that part of the refuse that is suitable for reuse. The experiments with household refuse mentioned above can be thought of as an attempt to test the market. Indeed, a certain amount of resources must be expended on expanding the market for refuse resources, as one cannot rely on the existent market to provide the necessary information and contacts: active marketing is necessary. Transaction costs must be reduced: that is the cost of spreading and utilizing information, and the costs of establishing contacts and contracts are currently too high.

It is not unreasonable to assume that firms try to avoid those activities which lead to losses. This implies that firms are interested in reducing the costs of production, including the cost of disposing of wastes. As the prices of raw materials and of traditional waste disposal methods have increased, firms have been more interested in reclaiming valuable raw materials in their waste products, thereby also reducing the total amount of wastes. As information on the feasibility of such projects is greatest within the firm, we would

expect that both of these problems would be studied by the same
department within the firm. It also seems natural to try and reduce
the corresponding social costs by establishing contacts between
firms.

Establishing a market for primary waste materials is one way of
reducing such costs. The prices on this market can be both 'negative'
and 'positive'. Negative prices imply that the firm is willing to pay in
order to rid itself of its wastes. The largest 'negative' price it is
willing to pay is the cost of traditional waste disposal methods. It is
the demand for the raw materials in the wastes that determine
whether the price will be positive or negative.

Assume that a number of firms are willing to deliver a certain
waste, S, to potential buyers. The amount that the firms are willing
to deliver at a given price is given by the line U. This price will
depend upon the costs of traditional waste disposal, transportation
costs and so on. Let us assume that the firms wish to dispose of q units
and are willing to pay for such disposal. (The price is negative.) The
buyers are prepared to accept the wastes proportionally to the price
paid them: if the price decreases, they are willing to accept less. (Line
CE in figure 20.) As can be seen in the diagram, the firms will not be
able to sell all q units; $q-q_1$ units will have to be disposed of by
traditional means. Thus q_1 units will be sold at the price p_1. This ar-
rangement benefits all parties involved. The selling firms gain p_1BA
– the difference between the costs of traditional disposal and the
amount they must pay to the buyers in order to be rid of q_1 units. The
firms that 'buy' the wastes – accept the negative price – gain a sum
corresponding to p_1BC: the difference between what they actually
are paid, and the least amount they were willing to accept (a sort of
reversed consumer surplus). Finally, under the assumption that the

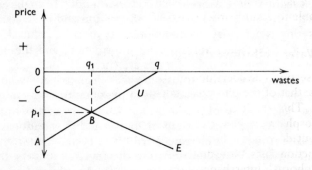

Figure 20 The determination of the price of wastes: negative prices.

price of traditional waste disposal corresponds to the true social costs, triangle *ABC* shows what society gains by the transaction.

Assume now that the price of the original raw material increases, thus increasing the demand for wastes containing this resource. The price of this waste may then become positive. Figure 21 illustrates this case, where p_2 is the equilibrium price. Note that the entire amount of wastes, q, is sold at this price. The selling firms gain p_2FqG, the buyers gain p_2FD, and society gains $DFqG$. (It is of interest to observe that society has a positive gain even with negative prices.)

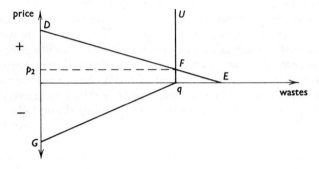

Figure 21 The determination of the price for wastes: positive prices.

Finally, we can expect that the increasing costs of traditional waste disposal methods and raw materials will lead to the establishment of a 'waste exchange' to reduce transactions costs involved. Further, society can, by taxing original raw materials, or by taxing traditional waste disposal methods affect the extent to this market. While recycling is, of course, not in itself a goal, it is one of many means available to attain particular social and political goals.

3.4 Water pollution: detergents and phosphate

This section considers one of the more widely debated ecological issues: that of the phosphate additives in detergents used to soften water. This problem has a number of interesting aspects: the amount of phosphate can be varied, other products can be substituted for it without decreasing the detergents' effectiveness, but changing the production costs. Note that while one uses the terms 'phosphate' and 'phosphorus' interchangeably, the phosphate additives contain about 25 per cent phosphorus.

3.4.1 The effects of the phosphate additives. The problem at
hand stems from the effect of phosphate as a nutrient: the introduction of this substance into lakes, rivers, and oceans changes the
conditions under which all marine life exists. The reproduction rate
of algae, for example, is dependent upon sunlight, temperature,
carbon dioxide, and the availability of food. While the first three
components are rather constant, the fourth can be varied by the
introduction of foreign elements such as phosphate into the water.
Lakes and oceans are slowly being choked by the increase in water
plant life, a process that is accelerated by the introduction of nutrients
such as phosphate. If we assume that 35 per cent of all phosphate
discharged into watersheds originates in detergents, can we then
conclude that this phosphate accounts for 35 per cent of the damage involved? Producers point out that as algae growth rates are
not proportional to the amount of phosphate in the water, and as
there are other sources of phosphorus in sewage water, forbidding
the use of phosphate in detergents would have but a marginal effect
and our lakes would continue to be plagued by abnormally high
levels of algae. As the water closet is not likely to be replaced within
the foreseeable future, the problem of phosphate, according to the
same producer, is best approached by sewage treatment.

   While these remarks hold for smaller lakes, they are not relevant
for larger bodies of water such as the Baltic or the North Sea. Here
we do not observe a decreasing effect with increasing phosphate
discharges. As all watersheds flow into the oceans, such reasoning
seems naive. It is apparent that we are confronted by two problems, a
biological one, and an economic one. The former concerns the
relationship between the phosphate and the growth of water plants;
the latter concerns society's evaluation of choked and lifeless bodies
of water. In the short run, we must weigh the advantages of using
our lakes as bathing places or as recipients of sewage; in the long run
we must consider the consequences of dead lakes and the various
possibilities of reclaiming them. During recent years, a number of
lifeless Swedish lakes have been restored almost to their original
condition. Preliminary calculations seem to indicate that the recreational value thereby created is in excess of the restoration costs.

   The economic aspect of the problem centers on the question of
prices: does the phosphate consumer base his decisions on correct
prices? Can he obtain via the price system correct information as to
the true social cost of his consumption, the costs of dead lakes as well
as sewage treatment costs?

3.4.2 Effluent charges. Given the problems of implementing effluent charges, the damage created by phosphate in sewage water is best reduced by attempting to tax phosphate earlier in the production chain. Such a measure would be but a partial control aimed at one of the larger contributers to pollution. Can we then impose a tax on phosphate in detergent that will cover both the increased costs of treating water containing phosphate and/or the damge to the environment caused by phosphate? Will such a tax result in the adoption of less damaging and less costly additives in detergents? We must be aware that a tax on but one component of detergents may result in new problems: the substitution of other additives with unknown environmental effects which may be just as undesirable, the increase in water use due to less effective detergents, and so forth.

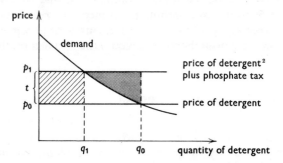

Figure 22 Demand for detergents.

The principles involved are presented in figure 22. The slope of the demand curve will depend on the possibility of other types of detergent being used when the price of those containing phosphate is increased. The increase in price from p_0 to p_1 due to the introduction of the effluent charge t leads to a decrease in consumption from q_0 to q_1.[2] The total revenue collected is tq_1, the shaded area, and is assumed to cover treatment costs. However, it is more interesting to consider the gains to society that stem from this tax.[3] The total social cost without the charge is p_1q_0, of which the producers bear p_0q_0, while the consumers of the environment bear the rest, $(p_1-p_0)q_0$, via higher effluent charges or accelerated entrophication in lakes. The social

[2] We assume constant marginal costs, thus forcing the consumers to bear the entire tax.
[3] We assume that the purification costs per unit of phosphate are the same as the environmental damage caused by discharging the same unit into a watershed.

loss without the effluent charge is shown in figure 22 by the dotted area; this loss is not balanced by any consumer surplus. One way to measure the effectiveness of any environmental policy, such as an effluent charge on phosphate, is to examine the policy's effect on this social loss. Further, with such a tax on phosphates, the social costs of the phosphate additives will be borne by the users of detergents, and not society as a whole. That is to say, the principle of 'the polluter must pay' is followed.

In theory, the revenue raised by the tax on phosphates can be used both to pay the increased treatment costs and to compensate those whose welfare is decreased by dying lakes. However, this type of compensation is difficult to implement. But even if the revenue is used only to improve sewage processing, municipalities will have a stronger incentive to improve environmental quality (an increase in the degree of purification results in an increased reimbursement). And the increase in price of those detergents with phosphate additives allows the consumer to understand the social costs that their actions cause.

3.5 Sulphur dioxide and air pollution

While many of the economic aspects of the problems created by sulphur dioxide are similar to those created by phosphates in detergents, the study of the SO_2 related problems can easily be related to other air pollutants. Even though the problem has both a regional and an international aspect, we will only consider the former. SO_2 in the atmosphere harms plant and animal life as well as causing extensive damage to various materials via corrosion. Some studies have indicated that the cost of this damage may be as great as 500 kronor per ton of SO_2 released into the atmosphere. In addition, while SO_2 causes human injury in both physical and psychological senses, this damage is extremely difficult to measure. This regional problem can be solved either by reducing the amount of SO_2 released into the atmosphere, or by building higher chimneys. Both methods fulfill the goal of reducing the concentration of SO_2 in the local atmosphere.

3.5.1 The nature of the problem. The most common approach to the sulphur dioxide problem has been that of direct regulation. The percentage of sulphur in fuel oil has been set at a certain level for Sweden as a whole, and at a lower level for the larger metropolitan areas. The Swedish report to the UN Environmental Conference in

1972 attempted to calculate the cost of reducing SO_2 emissions. The marginal costs presented had the approximate appearance of the *MC* curve in figure 23.[4] The costs for larger reductions increase rapidly. The second curve in the diagram is a hypothetical marginal willingness to pay curve, which assumes that this willingness is rather high for a reduction from 800 000 to 700 000 tons per year, and rather low for the reduction of the last 100 000 tons. If we assume that the precipitation of SO_2, which is partially dependent on emissions in other countries, is constant, the optimal reduction obtains where the marginal costs are equal to the marginal willingness to pay.

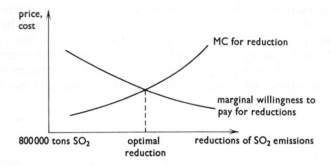

Figure 23 The determinant of the optimal reduction.

This reduction can be obtained either by using 'clean' oil (oil having a low sulphur content), employing another source of energy, or by reducing the SO_2 content in smoke. Regardless of the manner in which the reduction is achieved, a given reduction should always be obtained with the lowest possible costs. For example, let us assume that the current social costs of SO_2 emissions are 1000 kr/ton SO_2. That is 500 kronor as stated above, and 500 kronor for the damages that are not readily assigned an economic value. If the users of oil are to pay for the damage caused, the price of oil will have to increase by the additon of a 'pollution fee' of 10 kronor per ton for light oil and 42 kronor per ton for heavy oil.[5]

3.5.2 The instruments of environmental policy. If the goal of an environmental policy is to reduce SO_2 emissions, then we should examine the efficiency of the various means available to obtain this goal: the use of clean oil, the use of other sources of energy, the use of

[4] See Summary in SOU 1974:101.
[5] Light oil: 0.6% sulphur by weight. Heavy oil: 2.3% sulphur by weight.

higher chimneys, and the direct processing of smoke to reduce its
SO_2 content. Ignoring for the moment the global effects, our primary task is to force the users of oil to take into consideration the
social costs of their consumption. These costs vary with many
factors, including population density, the existence of production
processes that are affected by the SO_2 content of precipitation, and
the direction of the prevailing winds.

If we ignore administrative costs, the ideal set of effluent charges
can be obtained by environmental monitoring stations that are
coupled to measuring devices at the source of pollution so that the
relationship between SO_2 emissions and environmental damage can
be instantaneously measured.[6] These charges would probably be
different for differing locations within the region in order to reflect
the varying social costs at differing levels of pollution. Thus, given
unfavorable winds, 'price signals' would then suggest to the oil users
that they reduce their polluting activities either by switching to an oil
with a lower sulphur content, increasing their smoke purification or
simply by burning less oil. Thus every user would have economic
incentive to choose if not an optimally purifying process, at least one
that fulfilled certain stated 'standards'.

However such a solution is far from optimal when administrative
costs are included in our cost calculations. Other, less optimal but
more practical methods must be chosen, thus allowing the efficiency
of effluent charges and direct regulations to be compared. For example, one could monitor the emission levels of a polluter and make
a charge representing average costs (this charge could also be dependent upon weather conditions). The corresponding regulatory
measure would be to allow a certain amount of SO_2 emissions
during a given period. Another, less sophisticated method would be
to set the maximum permissible percentage of sulphur in the oil, and
allow only oil with no higher sulphur content to be used. This is the
method currently employed in Sweden. Note that this method gives
no incentive to users to process their emissions. Further, as this
method does not consider the effect of discharges on the environment, it is more difficult to adjust the standards to meet changing
local conditions.

3.5.3 A comparison of the various methods. It is common to
distinguish between the 'regulation' approach and the 'tax' approach
when studying environmental policy. We shall illustrate the differ-

---

[6] One could, in theory, replace the monitoring stations with a complicated mathematical model.

ence between these two approaches using SO_2 emissions as an example: the latter method is represented by a measuring device that adjusts the charge according to the damage caused by the discharges, the former by a meter that measures total emissions. With a few minor changes the 'regulation' approach can also be thought of as including measures that regulate the percentage of sulphur in oil consumed.

The first difference we shall mention is that of information and control. If one chooses to set standards, these should not be general but rather particular to each source of pollution, while at the same time maintaining a total level of pollution that is socially acceptable. Actually emission standards require a social efficiency study for each and every source of pollution, as one runs the risk of setting high emission levels for those who could cheaply remove the SO_2 from their smoke and vice versa. The marginal costs for reducing SO_2 emissions should determine the amount of the polluting activity allowed, as the following example demonstrates.

Assume that two equally large oil-burning power stations are located in a given region, and that they employ slightly different generating techniques. The older of the two has higher smoke processing costs than the other, as shown in figure 24. If a standard is set so that each plant must reduce its emission to q_0, the marginal cost for this reduction will be higher in the older plant. If we instead require a given total reduction, it would be profitable to reduce the emission level in the newer plant while increasing it in the older. This total reduction obtains at the lowest cost when the marginal cost for further reductions is equal in both plants. However, in order to choose q_1 and q_2 so that total costs are minimized, the regulatory agency must know the marginal cost curve for each plant.

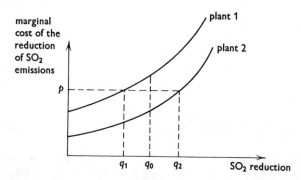

Figure 24 Regulatory solution.

By setting a tax on emissions, instead of a regulation, the minimal cost solution obtains automatically. In figure 24, if this tax were set to p, profit maximization would lead both firms to reduce their emissions to the socially desirable level. Note, however, that society can ensure an increase in welfare by setting the same tax for all plants only if the marginal damage caused by the plants' emissions is independent of the source of pollution. Assume that this is not the case, as shown in figure 25, where the damage caused by the older plant is the greater. If the same tax, a, is charged to both plants, the corresponding reductions will be q_1 and q_2. However, if the tax is set according to damages caused, plant 1 should reduce its emissions by q_1^* and plant 2 by q_2^*. Note that the reduction in plant 1 is greater than that in plant 2, a reversal of the result of an identical tax for both plants. Only if damages caused are similar for both firms should a single tax be set.

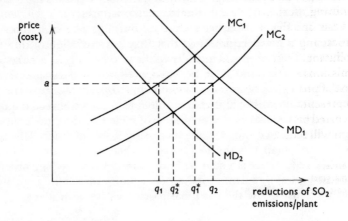

Figure 25 Different damages.

A combination of preliminary regulations and taxes can be used to find an optimal solution by trial and error. First the environmental protection agency (EPA) sets a tax on which the firms then base their reductions in SO_2 emissions. The EPA then observes the resulting total reduction. If a further reduction is desirable, the tax is increased; or, if the reduction is in excess of that required, the tax may be lowered. Such a process can result in a final position where the effluent charges correspond to the politically determined marginal willingness to pay. The only information required by the EPA is a measurement of the total emission level, and each firm is allowed to choose its own optimal production method.[7]

The above reasoning assumes that the EPA observes the level of emissions in one period and adjusts the tax in the next period in such a way that if the level of emissions is greater than desired, the tax is increased. If the difference between these two taxes is small, one expects a small reduction in emissions. However, as the example below shows, this need not be the case. The marginal cost curve is that appropriate for the reduction of the phosphate content of sewage water (see earlier sections). Assume initial conditions are such that with a tax a_z, the level of emissions is Y_z. Now consider the case where the EPA wants to make a small change in the emission level and expects to achieve this by a small increase in the tax to a_{z+1}. A quick glance at figure 26 suggests that the firm will reduce its emissions to Y_z^*, as between Y_z^* and Y_z the cost of processing the wastes (given by the MC curve) is less than the tax incurred by emitting them ($MC < a_{z+1}$). But inspection of the whole MC curve reveals another section between Y_{z+1} and Y_z^{**}) where the cost of processing the wastes is less than the tax incurred by emitting the pollutant. To take advantage of this would also involve eliminating emissions in the range Y_z^{**} to Y_z^* where the tax cost is lower than the cost of processing the wastes. If the cost saving between Y_{z+1} and Y_z^{**} (represented by the hatched area in figure 26) is greater than the cost incurred between Y_z^{**} and Y_z^* (represented by the dotted area), then the firm will reduce its output of the pollutant from Y_z to Y_{z+1} when the

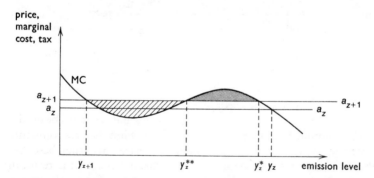

Figure 26 The emission jump.

[7] A problem occurs if differing reduction levels require differing investment in capital equipment to process the emissions. Such a trial and error method can lead to investment in equipment that is not optimal in the final position.

tax is increased from a_z to a_{z+1}. That is to say, a small change in the tax would trigger off a large change in the emission level. So emission levels between Y_z and Y_{z+1} may not be attainable by the tax method but would of course be attainable by setting standards.

The other basic difference between the two methods is their effect on the distribution of income. If the polluters are charged a fee, the revenue collected can be used to compensate those adversely affected by the remaining emissions. The regulatory method does not allow for such compensation but instead creates a 'pollution profit' which the polluter has a right to collect. This problem is illustrated in figure 27 for an activity such as residential heating where private and social costs are not identical. We assume that private marginal costs are constant over a rather large interval, and that social marginal costs are either increasing (case 1) or decreasing (case 2). The first case assumes that the marginal 'disutility' of pollution, increases as pollution increases, while the other assumes that disutility decreases with increasing pollution. This latter case implies that it is the initial pollution which causes the greatest discomfort, while continuing pollution causes less and less disutility.

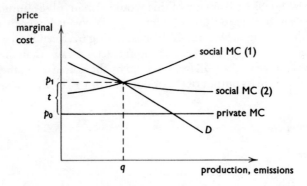

Figure 27 The two methods' effects on the distribution of income.

The optimal level of production and emissions occurs at point q where demand is equal to social marginal costs. This production can obtain either via direct control or a tax t that increases the price from p_0 to p_1. This latter method produces revenues tq. On the other hand, if the maximum allowable discharge is set at q units, the market price of the commodity will rise to p_1 in the new equilibrium position. This higher price implies that the firm receives an increase in profits – a 'pollution profit' – of $(p_1-p_0)q$, an increase which is identical to the revenue which could have been raised if an emission tax had instead been used.

An interesting question now arises: is the revenue from a tax on emissions sufficient to compensate those who are adversely affected by the pollution level that obtains after the firms have adjusted their production to this tax? The damage caused is represented by the area between the private and the social marginal cost curves. As can be seen in the diagram, if the social *MC* increases with increasing pollution, then the revenues collected are more than enough to compensate for damage caused. However, given a decreasing social *MC* curve, we find that the taxes collected are not sufficient to ensure full compensation. Only in the case where marginal damage costs are constant will the amount collected always be equal to the compensation necessary.

It should also be noted that setting a uniform tax per unit of emissions may result in some of the emitting firms being unnecessarily forced to shut down. This is illustrated in figure 28, where q_0 is the optimal level of output for which social marginal cost equals price. The tax rate t is determined by the difference between private and social marginal costs. This tax is applied uniformly on all units of output and so shifts the average variable cost (AVC) to AVC^*. The

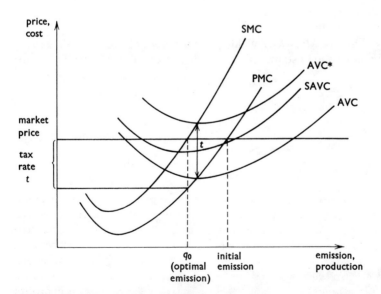

Figure 28 Differences in average variable costs.

firm is thus forced to shut down although its social average variable costs *(SAVC)* are less than market price. This is generally true if the private *AVC* curve excluding the tax *(AVC)* has its minimum point to the right of the optimal level of pollution (production). The resulting closure of these factories can, of course, be avoided if the tax is constantly adjusted so that it always corresponds to the value of the damage caused. However, such an adjustment process greatly increases administrative costs and can well have the unfortunate result that it is cheaper to allow some firms to close down, even though they would not be forced to do so given correctly formulated taxes.

As a uniform tax per unit is an alternative to a 'flexible tax'[8] the question naturally arises whether such a tax could result in an optimal solution if one was restricted to the use of marginal analysis. Consider, for example, water pollution where the marginal damage curve has a different appearance from that for air pollution. In the former case, the *MD* curve has a 'wave-like' form indicating that certain activities are no longer possible after a certain level of pollution is reached. In the following figure, the first peak could indicate that the water is too polluted to be used as drinking water, while the second could indicate a level of emissions which made bathing impossible. These wave-like effects are accentuated by the pollutants' effects on animal and plant life. We assume that the *MC* curve is decreasing.

The rule *MC=MD* yields these different optima (Y_1, Y_2, and Y_3) including an unstable one, Y_2. At this latter point, *MC=MD*, but any

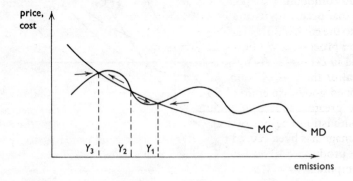

Figure 29 A non–convex *MD* curve.

[8] This tax is always equal to the value of the external effects.

change will result in a movement away from Y_2 in one direction or the other. It seems probable that the final position obtained will be either Y_3 or Y_1, both of which are stable. However, some sort of total evaluation of the area between Y_1 and Y_3 is necessary if one is to differentiate between the two (we assume that no fixed costs have changed). Thus a 'flexible' tax is no guarantee that a marginal analysis will produce a unique optimum.

3.6 Lead, and other non-biodegradable substances

This section will examine the environmental problems caused by lead and other substances such as the heavy metals and certain insecticides like DDT (which is used in agriculture to increase production per acre) that do not deteriorate in nature. It is characteristic of these substances that they are poisonous even in small concentrations. The widely publicized incidents in Japan where many hundreds of persons died from eating fish tainted with mercury, and rice containing cadmium aptly illustrate this point. Part of the problem lies in the fact that these substances accumulate in living organisms. The forms of pollution caused by different lead compounds have common characteristics and are of special interest due to lead additives in gasoline. The compounds are accumulated in vegetation and animals and thus affect a great number of the commodities we consume (see figure 2).

3.6.1 Lead emissions. It has long been realized that lead and various lead compounds are poisonous to animals and humans. In addition to that occurring naturally, significant amounts of lead are released into the environment each year as by-products from various production processes. We find lead in batteries, in paints, in metal alloys, and in ceramics. As by-products are not always reclaimed, a good deal of the wastes from the processes producing the above mentioned goods are emitted directly into the environment. However, the greatest source of pollution is the exhaust from the internal combustion engines of today's motor vehicles. And even though damage has been caused by lead from other sources (particularly in the production of lead and in other goods where lead is an important component as well as lead poisoning from ceramics containing lead) those caused by the exhaust fumes from automobiles are the prime reason that lead pollutants are now studied.

A large percentage of today's air pollution comes directly from the exhaust of internal combustion engines. Studies have uncovered up to 200 different chemical compounds in such exhaust gases with carbon monoxide (CO), hydrocarbons, and nitric oxide (NO), in that order, being the most plentiful. It was estimated that 1 000 000 tons of carbon monoxide, 150 000 tons of hydrocarbons, 50 000 tons of nitric oxide, and 2500 tons of lead compounds were emitted in Sweden in 1968.

Lead additives in gasoline originated in the United States where they have been in use since 1923. The lead compounds such as tetramethyl and tetraethyl reduce the 'knock' in engines as the compression ratio increases. It is cheaper for refineries to use these compounds to raise petrol's octane value than alternative methods currently available. The average Swedish automobile emits approximately one kilogram in one year of the inorganic lead compounds lead chloride and lead bromide in the form of small particles that are easily spread by the wind. Lead pollution originates not only in the exhaust but also from the crank case and from evaporation in the gas tank and the carburettor.

Even though, quantitatively, lead discharges are much smaller than others in automobile exhaust, it is just these emissions whose future effects are most uncertain. According to one of many different studies, a normal amount of lead in human blood is 0.1 to 0.5 ppm. At values greater than 0.8 ppm, symptoms of lead poisoning may well appear. It should be noted that had it not been for industrial uses of lead, these 'normal' values would be much lower.

One of the reasons for concern is lead's tendency to accumulate in the body. There is even a theoretical risk of genetic damage. American workers who have constantly been exposed to lead have a higher mortality rate than other workers. Note that the accumulation of lead in the body does not necessarily imply that one has inhaled exhaust fumes for many years. The lead content of vegetation along highways is abnormally high. Thus lead can enter the human body via milk produced from cows that grazed near highways.

While there have been no reported cases of lead poisoning caused by lead pollutants in the urban atmosphere, the limitations placed on the use of lead additive are justified by the uncertainty of future effects of a possible increase of lead in the atmosphere. For instance, present methods are unable to measure the organic compounds of lead in the body. Such compounds are ten times as poisonous as inorganic ones, but luckily are emitted mainly by evaporation from gasoline rather than from combustion.

3.6.2 The regulatory solution. One cannot isolate the problem of lead emissions from that of pollution by other substances in motor exhausts. Indeed, the most serious problem is probably caused by carbon monoxide, which represents about 80 per cent of total exhaust pollutants, rather than lead. As traffic within urban areas has increased astronomically during the past two decades, some solution to the problems created must be found. However, they have up to now defied all solutions.

The current approach is to try to reduce the pollutants in exhaust fumes to a more acceptable level. American norms have set the standards which the rest of the world has gradually adopted. The US standards for 1975 and 1976 models required that the carbon monoxide and hydrocarbon emissions be reduced by 90 per cent compared to the 1970 models, and nitric oxide by a corresponding amount compared to the 1971 models. To meet these standards, motor manufacturers will not only have to modify engines, but also install catalytic devices in the exhaust system to reduce pollutants. These devices, in turn, will more than likely require lead-free gasoline, as the catalysts are destroyed by lead. The questions to which we now address ourselves are how efficient are such emission regulations, and if it is feasible to introduce emission charges.

The greatest disadvantage with emission regulations is that they provide no incentive to reduce emission until the maximal boundary is reached. These can be interpreted in monetary terms to mean that all emissions below the maximum level are free, while those above it are exceptionally expensive. In the case of lead, the standard is set not according to the actual volume of emissions, but rather to dictate the greatest permissible lead content of gasoline. This standard does not give the petroleum industry any reason to reduce the lead content of gasoline until a new regulation setting a lower permissible level is adopted. Nor do such regulations stimulate the consumer to choose gasoline containing less than the permitted amount of lead.

A second problem with the regulations dealing with automobile exhausts is that the most recent ones apply only to the newest models. As a result, the full effect of any new regulation is not observed until all of the cars produced before it was set have been scrapped. Neither owners of older models nor the petroleum industry have any incentive to comply with the newest regulations until they are forced to do so. One wonders if there is some method available to force faster compliance with them.

3.6.3 The 'tax' solution. One method that is available is that of effluent charges. The problem we are here considering is similar to that studied in the preceding discussion of sulphur emissions in that it is not infeasible to set a maximum acceptable level for lead emissions during a given time period, and, by successive adjustments of the tax, gradually to approach this target value. As many countries have already set an upper limit on lead emissions, we shall turn directly to the much more interesting problem of the setting of the emissions tax.

The usual position taken in this case is that the tax should be proportional to damage caused. For example, if lead causes greater economic damage to vegetables than to trees, a person driving on a highway bordered by cultivated land should pay a higher tax than a person driving through a forest. However, if the taxes are not to require administrative costs in excess of efficiency gains, a system of differentiated charges is not feasible. As the technical relationship between lead in gasoline and lead in exhaust fumes is rather well known, the most appropriate tax seems to be one on the lead content of gasoline. There are, of course, variations in emissions depending upon the motor's construction and the manner of driving, but, again, differentiation along these lines is not practically possible. A tax on lead content will raise the price of gasoline so that relatively lead-free gasoline will be more attractive to the consumer. Assuming that motorists do not have a completely price inelastic demand for gas, a tax on lead content will provide an incentive for motorists to use gasoline with little or no lead additives.

It is not unusual that regulations and taxes are presented as two competing solutions to a given problem. In the case of lead these two methods are seen to complement each other: the tax on the lead content of gasoline provides the incentive to comply with the standard that the politicians have set. Here one uses the powerful economic incentive provided by the tax to obtain an acceptable emissions level set in reference to health standards.

3.6.4 The effects on product quality. Another problem created by persistent materials like the heavy metals is that they tend to accumulate in foodstuffs (via the ecological system). In the later stages of the food chain, such products can cause physical injury to man since they accumulate in the body. In some cases, the length of this chain can be very short indeed as is the case with lead additives in ceramics or silica dust in certain industries, a problem considered below.

From an economic point of view, the common denominator to the problems caused by the emissions of non-biodegradable substances is that the quality of the final product is adversely affected. Earlier sections have discussed how external effects caused by the partial nature of the price system could be controlled. However, in the case of these substances, the negative effects of emissions will be present long after all emissions have ceased due to earlier accumulation in land, water, and food chains.

In theory, this problem could be solved in the context of a perfect market economy: the perfectly informed consumer with a good understanding of physiology, hygiene, and organic chemistry would not be willing to pay the same price for vegetables or fish with differing percentages of DDT or mercury. However, such quality differences can only be discovered by using rather sophisticated instruments. It is also unreasonable to assume that any consumer could be an expert in so many different fields: the type of consumer necessary for the perfect market to function properly does not exist.

One way to reduce the information that a consumer must gather is to establish quality controls and perhaps to forbid commodities of very poor quality. These policies could be formulated in such a way that it would be apparent that one was utilizing the increasing returns that are obtainable in collecting, assessing and spreading information. It would thus not be necessary for every consumer to collect and analyse the information necessary to help him choose between two goods as this job would be done for him by some central authority acting as an ombudsman for him. Thus we can divide consumer decision making into two components: one performed by the consumer in choosing between an apple or pear according to his preferences, and the other performed by the more well informed ombudsman in collecting and processing information on product quality.

3.7 The working environment and resource allocation

The preceding has considered problems concerning the natural environment. In recent years, the concept of environment has been broadened to include other aspects such as the 'home environment' and the 'working environment'. This section will discuss some of the aspects of the latter.

It is not at all self-evident that the economic aspects of the allocation problems connected with the working and with the natural environment are similar. Indeed, to consider them both as 'environmental' problems is more of a hindrance than a help. There are however some indications that unconstrained market behavior does not produce an optimal working environment. We assume that the problem can be studied as a case of resource allocation where an improved environment increases the firm's costs and limits the prospects of increases in money wages. The job at hand is, then, to find an optimal mix of working environment and wage increases by considering both the workers' preferences as between job environment and wage income and the effect of the resulting increased costs on the firm's production. We should also point out that this discussion centers on imperfections of a different sort from those considered earlier.

3.7.1 Heterogeneous labor. Textbooks usually treat labor as a homogeneous commodity, or as one spread over a number of homogeneous markets with hours worked as the only variable quantity. This is, of course, only a simplifying assumption and there is no reason why labor cannot be considered an n-dimensional commodity. Seen from this point of view, it is apparent that many different types of working conditions can be included in the analysis of the labor market.

While it has not been formally demonstrated that equilibrium exists in the case where labor and other commodities are described as n-dimensional vectors, it is probable that the analogy between this type of market and the traditional one with one-dimensional goods is rather close. This would imply that equilibrium wages give a good approximation of the workers' preferences between the different aspects of the job and of the employer's ability to vary these conditions. It is of course assumed that both partners are fully aware of these different aspects and that wage negotiations are not exceptionally costly. If one job implied a higher risk of silicosis than another, we would expect that the more dangerous job would pay a wage high enough to compensate the employees for this added risk (this does not preclude the possibility that the wages would be so high that the firm would rather invest in protective equipment). There are thus strong *a priori* reasons to expect the market to generate an optimal mix of the different aspects of the job. In addition, as these aspects are all controlled by the employer – he can continuously compare the marginal costs of improving working conditions and the wage demands – and can all be negotiated, the problem is of a totally different type from that of the natural environment. (The effects on one firm of the working conditions of another should be considered one of pollution rather than one of working conditions.) From this point of view, there is no evidence that even a monopolistic firm that otherwise viciously exploits the laboring classes would provide a sub-optimal job environment in comparison to money wages.

Have we, then, created a problem that does not exist? The following sections try to show that contrary to Pangloss and Pareto, the market economy does not necessarily produce the best of all worlds. However, we must keep in mind that there are so many imperfections in the market that we will not be able to eliminate all, and that the correction of one imperfection with taxes on wages or consumption may well result in another imperfection somewhere else in the system.

3.7.2. The working environment and the tax system. It is not at all difficult to show that today's tax system tends to produce a better than optimal working environment. For example, if an employer must choose between spending extra on internal environmental improvements or on wage costs (when all wage and employment taxes are included, the total increase in money wages will be less than a krona), the employee must choose between an increase in after-tax wages by about 0.65 krona (depending on the marginal rates of the various taxes) or a bit more than a krona spent to improve the working environment (as a certain percentage due to depreciation allowances of investments are tax deductible for the firm).

That taxes are progressive can perhaps also explain why the working environment improves rapidly as one comes up the income ladder. It seems that consumption of the job environment is highly income elastic and this can partly explain the difference in working conditions for the highest and lowest paid groups of employees. Given an income elasticity greater than unity, we would expect that the working conditions vary more than wages. The effects of marginal tax rates heighten this variation. It does not require a subtle sociological theory of the wage structure to explain why executives have wall to wall carpeting at work but not at home as the carpeting purchased for the office has a much lower price than that purchased for the home.

3.7.3 The effects of wage bargaining. In the section on heterogeneous labor, we demonstrated how a perfect market could optimize working conditions provided that information and negotiation costs were low. In reality, these costs are exceedingly high. This heterogeneous nature of the labor market is by no means unique – the housing market exhibits many of the same characteristics – and leads to the creation of collective organizations which seek to reduce just these costs.

These organizations eventually lead to rather centralized wage bargaining and to the limiting of the number of tasks included in a given job. Wage negotiations dominate the bargaining sessions, and discussions of the working environment, if at all taken up, are assigned a secondary role. In many cases, the bargaining procedure followed today cannot find the optimal mix of environmental improvements and wage increases but rather tends to a *sub*-optimal working environment. Thus the increases in productivity are converted to money wages rather than investments in the working environment.

It is not unlikely that this bargaining system can also explain the differences in working conditions within the firm. While negotiations for blue collar workers are highly centralized, thus making substitution between wages and environmental improvement difficult, those for white collar employees are mainly individual negotiations where such substitution is easier. The tendency to suboptimal working conditions is greatest for those with the most centralized negotiations, and tends to decrease as one moves up the wage scale.

The last statement is reminiscent of one encountered in dealing with the natural environment. The working environment is much more collective for blue than for white collar groups. The conditions down mine shafts, on the factory floor, in the machine room are the same for all on the premises, while an executive's room is unique to him.

3.7.4 Insurance and incentives. The frequency and nature of industrial accidents and occupational diseases are dependent on the working environment. Only part of the hospitalization and compensation costs are borne directly by the employer on whose premises the injury occured. A similar problem is that of traffic accidents. Here indeed is a case of external diseconomies. As the current insurance policy premiums for such accidents and illnesses are proportional to a firm's wage sum, and as a differentiation of rates might well increase administrative costs so as to outweigh the benefits of differentation, we ask if there is no simple but more efficient set of rates available within the framework of the market economy. One such set is a series of bonuses similar to those for car insurance: such a system of rates would provide the incentive to the firm to take preventive measures to reduce accidents.

A closely related problem is that of the extent of the actual payment in relationship to the total amount of compensation. Most of the hospitalization costs of industrial injuries are paid by the social security system (that is, by proportional income taxes). By transfering these costs to an expanded job insurance system, the firm can be given an added incentive to promote job safety.

3.7.5 The problem of information. The model for optimal allocation assumed information to be complete and available without cost. If we abandon this assumption we can find welfare theoretic grounds for public intervention in the control of the working environment. A market economy tends to lead to sub-optimal research as a firm is is reluctant to bear the entire cost of obtaining knowledge that will most likely leak to other firms. The private gains are small compared to the social gains, but the firm pays the entire bill. As the private costs are essentially the same as the social costs, the state must finance much of the research if the optimal level of 'knowledge' is to obtain. Thus a public research program aimed at analyzing the working environment is as necessary as a program studying the natural one.

The communication of information is another aspect of the problem. One rather cheap way of spreading information is to have the public health authorities set standards or norms. In many cases, the use of rules of thumb will prove more efficient than more complicated rules based on expensive cause–effect studies.

3.7.6 The working environment and the age of the capital stock. Different studies have shown how the capital stock within an industry can be ranked according to age and productivity. There are usually only small possibilities for continuous substitution between labor and capital – the capital–labor ratio is more or less determined when the original investment is made. This implies that labor's productivity is set by the choice of capital equipment and that expanded employment is usually the result of new investments. Thus we expect that there will be some connection between the capital structure of an industry and its working environment, with the newer plants having the better environment. Thus substantial changes in the working environment will coincide with new investment or extensive reinvestment. It follows that it seems uneconomic to invest in a better working environment in plants having a capital stock which is nearly obsolete. Indeed, this is an argument which is also relevant to the natural environment: waste-processing capacity is often set in relationship to the age of the capital stock as is the case in the paper industry.

3.8 Some concluding remarks

In this chapter we have tried to apply the economic theory given in chapter two to some practical environmental problems of a familiar kind. The conclusions can be summarized in the following way.

(1) It is possible to find several environmental problems which can be solved at a lower social cost by using taxes rather than regulations.
(2) To obtain an optimal allocation of environmental resources by means of regulation requires more information than do taxes.
(3) The problems connected with valuing the externalities from pollution are the same whether charges or regulations are used.
(4) Although it is possible to reach the same solutions either by regulation or by taxes these two policy instruments have different influences on income distribution.
(5) The practical way of solving many environmental problems is to use a combination of several instruments e.g. regulations and taxes.
(6) The problems of the working environment are of a different nature from the 'ordinary' environmental problems especially with respect to the methods appropriate for their solution.

4

Environmental policy, an expanded perspective: organizational forms, economic systems, international implications, and restraints on growth

4.1 Introduction

In the first two chapters, we presented the general economic framework for environmental care and policy. We then used this basis to analyze a number of different problems in chapter three. In these discussions we have consciously ignored two rather important aspects: the appropriate size of the administrative areas, and the decision making process. The political decisions in most countries are made on various levels: ministries, bureaux, and municipalities. In principle, the higher up one goes in the bureaucracy, the larger is the area of jurisdiction connected with any one agency. Usually, the nature of the problem to be solved decides which section of the bureaucracy is responsible for solving it. However, as most problems connected with pollution have no clear-cut boundary, the present bureaucratic system may not be able to cope with it efficiently. In the following we address ourselves to this possibility.

Earlier chapters have assumed that pollution was but a marginal imperfection that could be corrected by a number of alternative policies such as taxes or regulations on the production and consumption activities causing the pollution. This concluding chapter will broaden our perspective both in time and place so that we can examine some of the assumptions behind our earlier analysis. The problems to be considered here can be grouped in four categories:

(a) As pollution is spread according to meteorological or hydrological forces, rather than the existing jurisdictional areas, environmental policy must be conceived in such a way that the 'correct' institution is found for each type of pollution.
(b) Is it possible that some alternative to the market economy, such as the command economy, will prove to be a more viable system for the solution of environmental problems?

(c) Certain environmental problems are global. Can we have a
     rational environmental care policy in a world economy that is
     organized so that each individual country is concerned mainly
     with its own problems and where effective international control
     agencies are lacking?

(d) Pollution is not limited in time. For example, as certain sub-
     stances accumulate in nature, their full negative effect may not be
     apparent for years. A closely related issue is that of natural
     resources which will be depleted sometime in the future. The
     current generation could approach these issues by maximizing
     its own welfare at the expense of coming generations' welfare as
     the latter have little or no influence on today's markets or politi-
     cians.

4.2 Regional aspects

Pollution does not stop at a region's national or international bor-
ders. Nor do the negative effects of pollution conveniently cease to
exist at these jurisdictional boundaries. The chances of implementing an effective environmental protection policy often depend on
whether the source of pollution is on the same side of such a boundary as the control agency. This problem is most acute when the
boundaries are international: one country has difficulty in enforcing
its laws inside another country.

A well known example is the sulphur dioxide emissions from firms
in the Ruhr industrial areas in Western Germany. Given unfavorable
weather conditions, these emissions are spread over the western
parts of Scandinavia where they increase acidity of lakes as well as the
air pollution in the area. Even though these countries wish to reduce
damage by limiting such discharges, they have almost no possibility
of doing so, as there is no binding international agreement on SO_2
emissions. While such examples abound, a similar problem occurs
within different jurisdictional regions of one country: a polluted
river that flows through a number of regions is an example of such a
case. Each of these regions is capable of affecting water quality to the
extent that each can exercise control over the sources of pollution. As
the damage differs from one region to another, these different
administrative areas do not all have identical policies to control the
sources of pollution under their jurisdiction. For example, a certain
region might suffer more from air pollution and therefore direct
most of its efforts to controlling this nuisance. Against this background, it is easy to appreciate that today's jurisdictional areas are

rather inappropriate for solving environmental problems. It seems advantageous to examine such problems in the context of special 'environmental interest regions'.

First of all, how should such areas be defined? As most problems of pollution are geographically bounded, any environmental interest region should be correspondingly designed. There are, of course, global problems such as DDT or the increase in CO_2 in the atmosphere due to the use of fossil fuels, but these are, fortunately, the exception rather than the rule. Ideal regions cannot be created without friction. As they should follow patterns set by hydrological or meteorological conditions, they will almost certainly not correspond to today's political regions. For example, as a relevant region for SO_2 emissions should be northwestern Europe, a commission to control such emissions would have to have the authority to cross not only national frontiers but also those set by COMECON and EEC. The pollution of the Baltic should be solved by establishing working areas containing the nations directly affected by the pollution. Needless to say, the chances of establishing such international regulatory bodies are not great. However, there is no reason to believe that such an institutional framework cannot be established within any given country. In what follows, we shall describe some of the economic and technological criteria that must be met if a region is to employ its resources efficiently. Even though not all of these conditions can be met in actual cases, they should nonetheless provide the basis for a more effective environmental policy.

4.2.1 Regional environmental protection agencies: a suggested organizational form. Regional control agencies should be created in such a manner that the vast majority of the effects of pollution occur *within* the region. This should not be taken to mean that all of the *sources* of pollution must lie in the region. Indeed, if the region is too large, losses in administrative and organizational efficiency may occur. Thus national or international bodies with a greater area of jurisdiction must be created to cope with interregional issues.

It does not seem impossible to create environmental protection bureaux that have their jurisdictional areas defined by, say, a watershed, where problems of water and air pollution can be approached simultaneously according to the regions' need for recreational areas. This principle has been adopted in the certain areas of the United States. For example, the Delaware River Basin Commission was created to solve water use problems of both a quantitative and qualitative nature (see section **3.3**). Similar agencies have been formed in West Germany, France, Holland, and England. The German Wasserverbände and the English River Boards are examples.

Such bureaux must have the authority to use all appropriate means to solve the area's pollution problems. In many countries, current environmental protection policy is based on more or less *ad hoc* principles. The Swedish environmental protection agency, which has judicial authority, examines firms' applications for permission to emit various pollutants. The result of such procedures is that the firm under consideration must process its wastes while other, older firms continue emitting the same wastes. Thus environmental protection bureaux should be given the authority to place charges on polluting activities. More than likely, these bureaux exhibit increasing returns to scale in such activities as water quality regulation, centralized waste disposal, and restoration of lakes and rivers. Efficiency gains can obtain by delegating to these bureaux the authority to use those means which are most efficient in each individual case.

Thirdly, the bureaux must set acceptable values for different environmental variables. For example, relevant variables in connection with water quality are underwater visibility, oxygen content, pH value, amount of coliform bacteria, and so forth. Similar variables for air and land quality should be set, as the latter is vital, especially for recreational purposes. Such variables can be difficult to set if they are closely related to ecological processes or must reflect long term goals. These target values should correspond to the preferences of the region's inhabitants as they are the most directly affected by any change in environmental quality. However, such efforts are hindered in that environmental variables lack an established market price. The optimal allocation of such public goods in practice is one of the unsolved problems in welfare economics. In our discussion of recreational resources, we suggested various alternatives to the usual allocation procedure according to political decision.

One final aspect of the topic should be mentioned: that of income distribution. We suggest that the bureaux should limit their attention when compensating those affected by environmental care policies to the relevant region, thus keeping the interregional transfer issue out of environmental policy.

4.3 National aspects of environmental issues

Regional environmental policy seeks solutions to environmental problems that are restricted to a certain geographical region. Such a decentralized policy has certain advantages over a more centralized approach. However, some environmental problems involve such a large area that regional solutions are not feasible, as the relevant region would be too small for efficient management. Such issues require national agencies for their solution, as they are best regarded as national problems. The exploitation of a certain resource, located in a specific region, but of vital national importance is an example of such an issue. Another is national parks and wilderness areas since visitors to such areas come from the entire nation. Indeed, most individuals appreciate the existence of such parks even if they never visit them. Further, wildlife research as well as cultural studies are dependent on such almost irreplaceable areas as these. Thus the preservation of these areas should be a nationally imposed constraint placed upon regional planning. Future generations are also dependent on national planning agencies.

Research into the environment is another aspect where increasing returns merit national planning. A good deal of today's research in this field not only in universities but also in private institutions is financed by central authorities. As the nation as a whole benefits from the results of such research, the national agencies should continue their support. Note that such central agencies can also aid regional ones in planning regional research programs.

Even though the regional bureaux set the detailed standards within their own territory, certain emissions must be regulated on a national basis. For example SO_2 emissions, the use of insecticides such as DDT, and the discharge of heavy metals must be controlled by national agencies. As SO_2 emissions cause damages over large regions, a national control agency will be the most efficient. It may choose to set an air-quality standard, or set an upper limit on emissions using the methods outlined in chapter three. Given a mobile source of pollution, such as the automobile, a national agency will again have advantages over a regional one. While some of the pollution problems connected with automobile exhaust are concentrated in the larger metropolitan areas, giving rise to various local regulations, the mobile source of emissions makes such regulations difficult to enforce. Centrally dictated norms such as requiring cleaner exhausts, limiting the amount of lead in gasoline, or restricting engine size need to be established.

Other pollutants that require national supervision are DDT and the heavy metals. The usual methods employed are the prohibition of the use of such substances. As the long range effects of these poisons are unclear, national control seems warranted.

4.4 International aspects

Many of the issues relevant when considering the decentralization of
national environment care bureaux into regional ones are as important in an international context. The main problem in decentralizing
national bureaux is that of defining areas of jurisdiction along geographical rather than political lines in such a manner that only small
amounts of the pollution of one area are spread to other areas. In
principle, problems caused by pollution should be solvable *within* the
region.

The boundaries of national states have not been created with
distribution of pollution in mind. Historians give many different
factors which have determined today's frontiers, but among these
are not patterns of rainfall or other climatic conditions. While there is
always a central authority within a country to set and enforce
environmental standards, such an authority is noticeably lacking in
international affairs. There is no court of last resort that can prevent
the spreading of pollutants over international boundaries or can
force one state to compensate another for damage caused.

The nature of the problem can best be understood in the context of
an example: the 'transnational' spreading of SO_2 from England and
the Ruhr to southern Scandinavia. Both England and Germany face
the same alternatives if they wish to reduce the damages caused by
SO_2 in their own countries: they can process the wastes to remove
SO_2 from smoke, they can use cleaner oil, or they can build higher
chimneys. This last alternative implies that the pollutants are
removed elsewhere by the prevailing winds, usually towards Scandinavia. This solution – higher chimneys – is also the cheapest for
these two nation states. If the damage caused in Scandinavia becomes
unbearable, these countries can always attempt to pay England and
Germany to choose one of the other alternatives. Such solutions are
possible only after long and trying negotiations: it is not self-evident
which country owns the air or in which direction the compensation
payments should flow. Given an international regulatory body that
could force the polluters to compensate for damage caused by their
emissions, such negotiations would become unnecessary. If
Denmark suffered damage caused by English emissions, when the
English chose to reduce their pollution problems by building higher
chimneys, then the regulatory body would force the English firms to
compensate the Danes.

Attempts have been made to resolve such conflicts. Several countries including Sweden have established special commissions to deal

with such international environmental issues. Sweden is attempting to reduce the pollution in the Baltic and Oresund via negotiations with the other nations bordering these bodies of water. OECD has also established a special environmental care commission. The United Nations has a number of organizations that attempt to solve such problems: ECE, WHO, ECOSOC, and FAO to name but a few. GATT has attempted to solve conflicts arising from the international spreading of pollutants. This implies that GATT must resolve trade conflicts – like import restrictions – created by different countries employing different environmental care policies. These organizations also aid in negotiating 'environmental treaties'. However, the most usual arrangements are either bilateral agreements or international conventions where the signatories bind themselves to follow a certain policy – e.g. not dumping wastes into the seas.

4.5 Environmental policy and economic systems

The preceding chapters have discussed the issues in environmental care policy in the context of a market economy, and have led us to accept that one of the causes of pollution is that environmental resources are not optimally allocated by the market mechanism. The principal reason behind this market failure is that many environmental quantities are public goods. Another aspect of the same problem is that it would be too expensive for the market mechanism to allocate these resources. In order for this mechanism to work, all goods and resources must be owned by someone. Further, it must be possible to establish binding contracts on both the buyer and the seller on matters of prices and quantities. The high transactions costs that would be associated with environmental resources perhaps explain why the market does not include them. Thus environmental care policy in a market economy is restricted to guiding production and consumption activities indirectly towards those activities that produce an optimal allocation of environmental resources. It has been claimed that there is a direct connection between our current economic system and the scope of, as well as the solution to, the problem of pollution. In particular, people have attempted to connect the market system – with privately owned, profit maximizing firms – and the scope of today's environmental problems; and to then use this connection to advocate the establishment of an entirely different economic system such as a command economy.

The Swedish economist Assar Lindbeck has classified economic

systems according to their different characteristics or dimensions.[1]
His ideas are outlined in figure 30, where we have also shown how
three different economic systems are described by the characteristics
he presents: Sweden, illustrating a market economy, the Soviet
Union, illustrating a command economy, and Yugoslavia, representing a socialist market economy. We intend to use this diagram as
a starting point in our discussion on how the choice of economic
system affects environmental care policy.

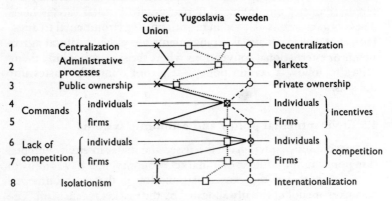

Figure 30 Different economic systems in profile.

It must be pointed out that there is a connection between the level
of development and the level of pollution. Given a limited industrial
sector, the wastes produced will also be limited and cause at most a
local problem. As the country develops the amount of wastes discharged will of course increase[2] and the problems of pollution will
increase in scope and perhaps distribution.

Further, we must recall that both technology and many environmental problems are largely independent of economic systems. The
percentage of sulphur in oil or phosphorus in human excretion
neither increases nor decreases as one changes from one economic
system to another. The difficulties in establishing rights to the air or
the problems associated in incorporating this resource in a market or
command system are also technologically given. The direction of the
winds or the flow of water in a river is not dependent upon what
economic system the air or water pass through. We have shown how

[1] Assar Lindbeck, 'The many dimensions of economic systems', *Ekonomisk Debatt*,
 1973:1 (in Swedish).
[2] Both the quantity and the quality of these discharges are important.

pollution can be controlled by different types of corrective action. The problem at hand, then, reduces to examining which economic systems, defined by the relationships on the commodity markets, are best adapted to solving those special problems arising from the allocation of environmental resources.

Lindbeck presents each dimension as polar opposites which imply some sort of scale. Thus economies can have different degrees of centralization as well as different ownership patterns. No actual economic system is so polarized that it would lie on the extreme right or left of the diagram. However, many western European countries lie, on average, definitely to the right of the eastern European command economies. We shall now examine how these different dimensions affect the use of environmental resources.

4.5.1 Decentralization vs centralization. If one accepts the hypothesis that pollution is caused by market failure or by the impossibility of creating markets for environmental resources due to their public nature, then it follows that economic systems with decentralized decision making in firms and households are inferior to those based on centralized decision processes with respect to the allocation of environmental resources. The market may fail to deal adequately with pollution since firms and households do not consider all aspects of their actions on environmental resources.

So an effective environmental care policy demands some form of centralized decision making to correct individual behavior. However, there is no inherent contradiction between highly centralized decision processes where environmental resources are concerned, and highly decentralized decision processes where other goods and services are involved. This issue was studied from a different perspective in an earlier section where we showed that the ecological regions that would lead to a more effective environmental care policy seldom correspond to the actual political structure of a country. Thus the centralization necessary for efficient environmental actions may be very different from that created for other purposes.

Even if extensive empirical evidence is lacking, it seems reasonable to assume that countries with centralized decision making can more easily create the type of organization necessary for an efficient environmental policy than a country with strong *laissez-faire* traditions and a political mistrust of central authority. Differences in economic systems, seen from this angle, appear to be more differences in attitudes than in the system itself.

4.5.2 Markets vs administrative processes. The next dimension is
that of administrative processes (which imply an increase in centralization), as an alternative to the market as a means of arriving at a
socially optimal environmental care program. On the extreme market side, we should note that firms and households receive insuffi-
cient information from the price system on the environmental
impact of their actions. If one replaces markets by administrative
processes and centralized calculations one can in principle perform
the necessary efficiency calculations on which a rational environmental care policy must be based. However, the step from theoretical calculations to an effective bureaucracy is a large one. The
command economy has of course the means available to solve the
problem, but one wonders if a bureaucracy created to make traditional production decisions can at the same time solve for and
implement an optimal environmental policy. The information required for such a task would be so extensive that it is probable that
environmental considerations would be lost in the bureaucratic
maze. It is much more rewarding to try and combine the market
economy with those centralized decisions necessary to protect the
environment.

4.5.3 Private vs public ownership. It is important to note that this
dimension is independent of the two preceding ones. There is
nothing self-contradictory in market socialism where the means of
production are publicly owned but production decisions are decentralized and resources distributed via market processes. Neither is
private ownership incompatible with centralized decision making,
as the German experience during the second world war demonstrated.

In the context of environmental policy, the concept of ownership
is important in discussion of issues connected with air, water, and
soil. The problems in establishing ownership rights to these
resources are no less in an economy with public than with private
ownership: water and air have the characteristics of public goods in
both cases. The environmental impacts of production can be
described as an encroachment on an area where somebody else has
ownership rights. The technical aspects of this encroachment are
independent of the type of ownership: a sonic boom is just as
upsetting if the land is publicly owned. On the other hand, ownership patterns do play an important part in corrective environmental
policy.

Even though it may be impossible to establish the complete

ownership rights, which would enable one to forbid access, there is a weaker right, that can be established. This would mean that a firm has permission to, or at least is not prohibited from, discharging its wastes into the air or water. If environmental policy is changed so that such discharges become illegal, then this discharge right is withdrawn. The firm that has lost this right will more than likely demand some form of compensation. Firms in many countries act as though they had a private right to discharge into air and water resources; the withdrawal of this right is a pretext for demands for subsidies. In theory, this private discharge right will not hinder the implementation of an optimal environmental care policy; the issue is really one of ownership and wealth distribution. One can avoid excessive claims for compensation from those with discharge rights by placing a time limit on these rights and by transferring future discharge rights to a public body. This agency may, of course, sell these rights.[3]

Those ownership and discharge rights connected with resources other than environmental ones have in all but two cases little effect on a planned environmental care policy. One of these cases concerns the difference between publicly and privately owned natural resources and is considered in detail later on in this chapter. The other concerns the possibility of internalizing externalities given different ownership patterns. If one and the same firm owns all of the productive units along a river it soon realizes that it cannot discharge unprocessed wastes into the river without decreasing total production. Thus if one person owns all of the productive units in an area, it becomes easier to discover and correct external diseconomies, as long as it is possible to calculate all such effects within the ecological region.

4.5.4 Incentives vs commands. These issues have been rather closely examined in the previous chapter where we considered the difference between effluent charges and regulations. In an economic system where almost all technical information is decentralized, it is not unreasonable to assume that the public authorities would prefer to employ economic incentives to obtain environmental policy objectives rather than issue direct production orders and levy fines for noncompliance. However, experience has shown that the most decentralized market economy tends to take a large 'step' towards

[3] A discussion of discharge rights is to be found in J. H. Dales, *Pollution, Property and Prices*, Toronto 1970.

the left of the diagram (towards 'commands') when questions of environmental policy are discussed.

Another aspect of this issue is whether it is possible to alter consumer and producer behavior: can an environmental 'cultural revolution' succeed in making economic agents aware of the environmental impact of their actions? We have considered this possibility in connection with our discussion on returnable drink containers, where we concluded that a campaign to persuade households to use only returnables and to actually return the empties could be successful. After all, such actions do not entail much extra effort on the part of households. It is presumably much more difficult in other areas where the difference in returns to privately profitable and socially acceptable behavior is greater.

From time to time the political debate on environmental issues concentrates on incentives and it is sometimes suggested that environmental problems can be solved only if we can create altruistic economic agents. It seems unnecessary to dwell on this point as all efforts to implement such a change in the incentive structure have failed except in the case of more or less simple matters, such as a campaign temporarily to reduce the use of electricity. If the amount of social cooperation that the economic agents are willing to extend is limited, it is best to direct what cooperation is shown to those areas where it can be most effectively employed. Further, any attempt to alter incentives towards altruism will create a substantial information problem. Altruism implies that every firm would include its effects on other firms and individuals in its cost calculations. However, such calculations would only be feasible if the firm had access to information that even a governmental environmental protection agency has difficulty obtaining. Thus the market system would lose much of its decentralized character and one would replace the incentives created by effluent charges (or regulation) with a very expensive system indeed.

The question of competition vs non-competition has been discussed above. The size of the problem is so large that we feel it merits its own section. In conclusion, we would like to point out that the above discussion is independent of a country's current institutional framework. It is not self-evident that an economic system with a large degree of centralization, administrative planning, public ownership and regulation is in a better position to solve its environmental problems than one to the right of it in the diagram: the issues seem to be the same in all economic systems. However, any attempt to solve environmental problems will imply a step to the left of the diagram as far as this issue is concerned, with or without a corresponding step where other allocation problems are involved. The use of effluent charges and the assigning of ownership rights over environmental resources are two examples of corrective policies which may be pursued.

An economic system based on altruistic incentives and complete environmental awareness is an unrealizable utopia, that may not even be desirable because of the resources that have to be expended in producing information. Everyone will naturally have a better environment, but it will be at the cost of other goods and services that also contribute to economic welfare.

4.6 Environmental care in an international setting

An important aspect of the question of pollution is its international character. As we have neglected this part of the problem in our earlier discussion, we shall here consider it in detail. This problem has some aspects which we have discussed earlier. For instance, conflicts will probably arise between the economic and political structure of nation states and the needs of ecological regions that do not coincide with national boundaries. This implies that we can apply our earlier analysis to the issues in an international setting. One new problem that does arise concerns international trade. What will be the effect of natural environmental care policies on international trade and the division of labor among nations? To what extent will the welfare in underdeveloped countries be affected by the environmental care policy programs in the industrialized nations? Is international cooperation in environmental issues necessary if disruptions in trade are to be avoided? These and similar questions have been debated in various international organizations.

We shall center our discussion around two groups of problems connected with the pollution produced by certain production and consumption activities.[4]

GROUP 1 Pollution is a local or national problem, but the goods produced by the polluting activities are traded on international markets and can be produced in any number of different countries. The location and scale of production in any one country depends among other things on that country's environmental care policy.

---

[4] We consider only pollution issues. Environmental problems connected with the recreational opportunities offered by wilderness areas within one country to citizens of another are similar to those discussed above (section **3.1**).

GROUP 2 Pollution is not only a national but an internaional problem as the pollutants are transported by air or water to
other countries. There are varying degrees of pollution,
ranging from one country's polluting of a body of water
that is bordered by a few other countries to the pollution
of the oceans or the global atmosphere.

Pollution problems belonging to group 1 have their greatest impact
on trade and perhaps lead to a harmonization of different countries'
environmental policies. However, as our later discussion will
demonstrate, such harmonization is not always desirable and can
actually result in a suboptimal allocation of environmental resources.
As might be expected, pollution problems of a transnational character are exceedingly difficult to solve, especially as the number of
countries involved increases. While nations sharing a common body
of water can more or less successfully agree on a common policy to
reduce pollution, effective global agreements are almost impossible
to negotiate. In both cases, a transnational environmental protection
agency with the power to enforce treaties is lacking, and the negotiations connected with environmental issues are usually very tricky
ones.

A fascinating problem that we can but superficially consider arises
in connection with transnational pollution and international trade. A
country that imports commodities whose production processes emit
wastes that are then spread to other nations may well contribute to
this pollution. Indeed, under unfortunate circumstances, it may be responsible for an increase in the damages to itself caused by such pollution. Thus part of the SO_2 that the winds transport to southern Sweden
is a by-product of the production activities that provide some of the
goods that Sweden imports from Germany and England.

The simultaneous flow of goods and pollution demonstrates that
the classical free trade argument that free trade leads to an optimal
resource allocation between countries is incorrect. One can demonstrate that a system of tariffs that discriminates against those countries producing transnational pollution yields higher welfare than
does free trade. However, such tariffs are probably not feasible in
practice, as they imply high tariffs for neighboring countries but low
tariffs for distant ones whose discharges never reach the importing
country.

4.6.1 Pollution and international trade. We shall now turn our
attention to the first group of problems, and will center our discus-

sion on a simple trade model illustrated in figure 31. This diagram presents a marginal cost curve for an industry that produces primarily for export. In addition to the usual factors of production, this industry uses an environmental resource – say the absorption capacity of a river – that lacks a market price. This implies a difference between the private and social marginal costs. Note that, for simplicity, we do not consider waste processing. The country is small, and the world price level determines the domestic price, p_0 in the figure. The country's own demand for the product is represented by the usual demand curve, and, given prices, home consumption will be q_0 units. If environmental costs are not considered, the total production volume will be q_2, of which $q_2 - q_0$ units are exported. If the industry is forced to consider social costs as well as private, optimal production will be q_1 units, of which $q_1 - q_0$ units are exported. It is clear that q_1 is the optimal production, as, with a production volume of q_2 units, society incurs a loss corresponding to the shaded triangle *BCD*.

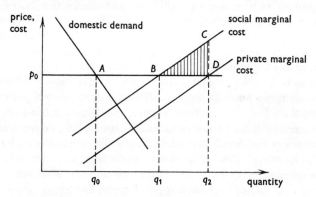

Figure 31 A polluting activity given world prices.

There are two aspects to the problem of trade and pollution. The first concerns the long term optimal distribution of labor and trade, while the second concerns adjustment when new effluent charges are set.

Environmental costs are just as real as any other costs and must be considered when studying the international division of labor. A country with relatively high environmental costs (e.g. due to a high density population), environmentally aware consumers, or a low absorptive capacity of the recipient media, will probably not have a comparative advantage in production activities that are highly polluting.[5] Thus if each country takes its own environmental costs into consideration in production decisions, an optimal international division of labor and international trade volume will obtain.[6] Production will occur in those countries where the total costs, including both the traditional factor costs and the environmental costs, are at a minimum. High environmental costs in one country may be compensated for by low labor costs. Thus those who claim that production should always take place where environmental costs are lowest are wrong. On the other hand, it is correct to maintain that a country with increasing incomes will find their environmental costs rising and their comparative advantage in production processes that impose large damages on the environment will eventually disappear. Only if other costs are identical will environmental costs alone determine the location of an industry.

If one accepts the argument that high environmental costs reduce a country's comparative advantage, then one also can understand why the imposition of identical effluent charges in all countries cannot be an optimal policy. Such a policy would imply that too great a percentage of production requiring large amounts of environmental resources would be located in countries with high environmental costs. On the contrary, one would want such production to migrate to countries with low environmental costs. The distribution of labor is not *a priori* suboptimal if some countries have more environmentally damaging production or a different environmental policy than others. This line of reasoning exposes the fallacy behind the claim that underdeveloped countries should have the same environmental standards as the developed ones. This policy would not allow the former to exploit their comparative advantages in the production of more environmentally demanding commodities. We have here the same sort of fallacy that often appears in the discussion of labor costs and international trade; i.e. that countries with high labor costs should protect themselves against competition from countries with low labor costs by placing tariffs on goods produced in those countries.

Our main conclusion is that, given the absence of transnational pollution, a global optimum obtains with free trade if each country pursues that environmental care policy which is optimal for that country. Tariffs and import restrictions directed against countries with lower environmental standards will lead to a distortion in the optimal division of labor and a welfare loss for all. Differing

[5] Note that we have assumed that pollution is local rather than transnational.
[6] See Södersten, *International Economics*, chapter 2, London, Macmillan, 1970.

environmental costs must be allowed to determine the location of industrial plants.

Is it then necessary for these various countries to cooordinate their environmental policies, or can the optimum obtain if some countries use regulation while other prefer taxes? The answer is that as long as the countries follow an optimal policy, the means which they use to achieve it are immaterial as far as the optimal international allocation is concerned. In figure 31, as long as the country produces at the optimal level, q_1, only the national distribution of income is affected by choice of policy means, a point already considered in chapters two and three.

The situation becomes more complicated if one country pursues an optimal policy, but others do not. The country with the more advanced environmental care policy may then place tariffs on imported commodities produced by the polluting firms in the non-optimizing countries. Such tariffs will increase welfare in the exporting countries at the expense of that in the importing one. The net result may well be an increase in total welfare resulting from a tariff, a conclusion which is rather surprising in international trade theory. These tariffs must be interpreted as one country's attempts to force other countries to face environmental costs.

Naturally, such a tariff policy would be extremely difficult to implement. How is one country able to determine if another is following an optimal environmental care policy? It is, after all, only the home country that can efficiently estimate its own environmental costs as environmental resources are public goods. For one country to question another implies that the country whose policy is questioned is unable to manage its own affairs. And such a point of view usually makes international negotiations difficult. Environmental policy must be determined by the country itself.

4.6.2 A model with two countries and one commodity. We shall now expand the model to include a second country but retain the assumption of a single good whose production also causes pollution. While the commodity is traded between the countries, the pollution created by its production remains in the country of origin. In the initial position, neither country pursues an environmental care policy, so that both countries' firms consider only the private costs in their environmental planning. Assuming D_1 and D_2 to be the countries' demand functions, and that their respective private marginal cost curves, PMC_1 and PMC_2 are as presented in figure 32, the countries are in equilibrium at price p_0. Given this price, consump-

tion in country 1 will be q_3, production q_1, with the difference, $q_3 - q_1$, being imported. This difference is equal to the quantity exported, $r_3 - r_1$, by the other country as long as we assume there are no other trading partners available.

If both countries simultaneously adopt an optimal environmental care policy and thus force both firms to reckon with social as well as private costs, a new equilibrium with a higher price, p_1, will be established. Country 1 will reduce its production and consumption

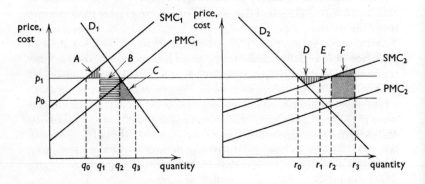

Figure 32 Two countries, single commodity.

to q_0 and q_2, while country 2 will also reduce both variables to r_0 and r_2. As the figure stands, country 1 will still be the importing country, but if the difference between the social costs of production and the private costs were much greater in country 2, it is possible that country 1 would become the exporting one. Note that imports, $q_2 - q_0$, are once again equal to exports, $r_2 - r_0$. As both countries have simultaneously changed policy, the welfare calculations are rather tricky. Country 1 experiences a welfare loss according to the area under the demand curve from q_3 to q_2 – the loss in consumer surplus (triangle C). The consumers in this country had been paying a price that was subsidized by those forced to live with the negative externalities in country 2. Country 1 experiences a further loss in that it must now pay a higher price for the goods it still imports ($q_2 - q_1$) in spite of the change in policy. In order to obtain equilibrium in its total foreign trade, country 1 is forced to increase production of some other good as its terms of trade have worsened: imported commodities have risen in price relative to exported ones. This loss is represented by the rectangle B. Finally, the country produced $q_1 - q_0$

fewer units and imports them instead. However, this change represents a welfare gain. While the price of the good has increased, the original producers did not pay the social cost of their activities. Thus the net gain is triangle A, that is, the area under the SMC_1 curve from q_1 to q_0 minus the price paid for this amount. This welfare change in country 1 will more than likely favor those who suffered from the earlier pollution at the expense of those who produce and consume the commodity.

The situation is entirely different for country 2. First of all, as earlier production implied that social costs were greater than income from the market, a decrease in production from r_3 to r_2 results in a definite social gain (area F). Once again, those who suffered from pollution will benefit most. As the price has increased, the country receives a higher price for its exports, represented by the areas E and D. That is, the country receives an income increase in excess of costs (area E) on remaining exports, as well as a higher price on goods that were previously consumed but are now exported that exceeds both costs and the amount the consumers are prepared to pay for the good (area D). The exact distribution of these gains among producers, consumers, and those directly affected by pollution depends largely upon the means used in the environmental care policy.

The gains to both countries are apparent, but the possibility of a net loss in one country cannot be excluded. Such a case would arise for an importing country which had been paying a price subsidized by those forced to live with the pollution in the exporting country.

Consider next the case where one country, say the first, unilaterally introduces an optimal environmental policy, while the other country continues to allow its firms to ignore social costs. This case is illustrated in figure 33. The equilibrium price will rise from p_0 to p_1 and total consumption will decrease. However, if there is a large gap between social and private costs, country 1 will experience an increase in imports in spite of the decrease in consumption. Thus the importing country will gain as the scope of the environmentally damaging production is decreased (triangle A) but experiences losses due to worsened terms of trade and decreased consumption (rectangle B and triangle C). The exporting country experiences (unknowingly?) a loss as damage to the environment increases with increasing production (F) but this loss is partly offset by the rise in price and the improved terms of trade (areas E and D). Note that one cannot preclude that the net effect on the environment may be a negative one: that the increased damage in the exporting country may exceed the decrease in the importing one. There is, however,

another dimension to this problem: the possibility that the importing country – the one that adopts an optimal environmental policy –
can avoid worsened terms of trade by introducing tariffs, and thus
creating a difference between what the home country consumers pay
and what the exporting firms receive. But a discussion of different
combinations of trade and environmental policies would take us too
far afield. Suffice it to say that the problem becomes rather complicated when world prices depend upon one country's environmental
policy. Further, if the country under study is a small one with but a
small percentage of total world trade then the assumption of
exogenous prices is not unrealistic and the model in the previous
section is sufficient. If, on the other hand, one wished to study the
EEC's or the USA's policy problems, then the more complex model
is required.

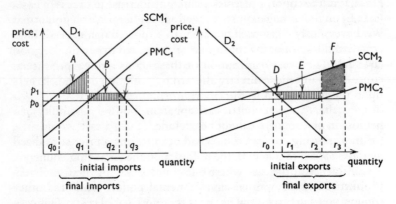

Figure 33

One must also realize that environmental policy can be formulated
to support trade restrictions. This is particularly likely to happen
when the products in question aid in the transnational dispersion of
pollution. An example would be the strict regulation of the DDT
percentage in foods that many industrial countries have introduced.

In the short run, there is also a direct connection between
environmental policy and the international currency system. As
shown above, if a country unilaterally adopts an optimal environmental policy, its terms of trade will worsen. Naturally, in the long
run, the country will reallocate its resources so that less of the
commodities that create pollution will be produced and correspondingly more of other goods. Such a reallocation means that labor will

have to be moved from one sector to another, a process that is made must easier by a system of flexible exchange rates and the *de facto* depreciation that will occur. (The currency must be overvalued in terms of other currencies as environmental costs have been neglected.)

If the exchange rates are fixed, on the other hand, this long term adjustment is more difficult as the balance of trade will worsen as imports rise and exports fall. The necessary reallocations can be obtained if effective demand is reduced and the rate of inflation is lowered below that of the rest of the world, but such a process is painful. Finally, we should note that the adjustment process can be shortened by an active labor policy whereby workers are given financial incentives to retrain for jobs in the expanding sectors.

4.6.3 Transnational pollution. One of the most serious threats to today's international economic structure is transnational pollution. We have shown that pollution that is limited to one area can be efficiently dealt with by a carefully planned environmental policy, and that the necessary regional environmental protection agencies either exist, or can easily be created. Such policies are not always friction free: one group will gain and another lose as the agencies seek to reduce the environmental damage caused by the production of goods that are sold abroad. As long as these groups live in the same country, it is always theoretically possible for the winners to compensate the losers. But if the groups affected by environmental policy live in different countries, serious problems can arise. These problems are, however, usually of little consequence for small countries involved in but a small percentage of world trade. Transnational pollution that is dispersed by water and air currents is, however, an exception. Take, for example, the problems arising from the transnational aspect of SO_2 emissions, which arise as the SO_2 particles remain airborne for several days and can thus be transported many hundreds of miles from their source. When the particles finally settle, they increase the acidity of lakes and soil. It has been calculated that half of the sulphuric acid which falls on Scandinavia originates as SO_2 discharges in England and Germany. And if this precipitation is to be reduced, the emissions must be reduced at their source.

There are several alternative policies available to cope with this issue. Perhaps the easiest one is for the affected countries to simply accept the level of transnational pollution and attempt to reduce emissions in their own countries. However, it may well be cheaper to pay the foreign polluters to reduce their discharges: the consumers

of the Scandinavian environment would in effect pay the polluting
West German and English firms a subsidy if they would reduce the
level of their discharges. A third alternative would be to force these
firms to pay effluent charges or to comply to certain environmental
standards set by the Scandinavian countries. Such a policy seems
more utopian than realistic.

The English and German authorities have no reason to force their
firms to adjust their production because of the damages their emissions inflict on other countries. The representation of pollution as
external effects is thus formulated. In an international setting regulatory commissions are lacking and any improvements must stem
from negotiations between countries. And countries lying down-
wind or downstream from sources of pollution in other countries
must bargain from a very weak position. More than likely they will
end up 'bribing' the firms to reduce their discharges.

The case is somewhat different if the countries inflict damage on
each other or if the polluted bodies of water or air can be regarded as a
common resource. Here other solutions are feasible such as an international treaty that limits total discharges and assigns quotas to each
country. Such agreements do exist in other areas; the fishing quotas
in territorial waters or the international agreements to prohibit the
dumping of certain substances in the oceans belong here. Such
treaties (actually environmental standards in an international context) are, however, notoriously difficult to enforce.

Effluent charges are also conceivable in an international environmental care program. The aim of such policies is, of course, to obtain
the same environmental standards that would have existed if the
polluted area was internal to some country. One possible approach
would be to allow some international 'environmental firm' to control the resource and give it the power to levy such effluent charges as
would be economically defensible. That is, the firm should maximize the present value of the resources with respect either to the
consumers in the affected countries or to the firms wishing to use the
resource. There would remain the question of the international
distribution of wealth, but this could be embodied in the shares in the
firm that the various countries owned. Similarly, the recreational
resources must somehow be distributed between these states. But
even if the creation of such a firm would not resolve all issues, at least
it would make people aware of their existence.

The creation of such a firm could also be the answer to pollution
problems more limited in scope. For instance, a firm, call it the Baltic
Water Agency, could be established to deal with the damages caused

by the discharge of raw oil in the international waters of the Baltic Sea. In concrete terms, every tanker that operates within the Baltic would have its cargo marked by radioactive isotopes so that discharges could be identified. Once an oil spill is discovered, the ship that had discharged the oil would be billed by the Baltic Water Agency according to the damage caused. Such transactions could be most efficiently handled if every tanker paid an environmental deposit that was repaid to the ship's owners after damage caused, if any, had been paid for. This deposit should be accompanied by an insurance policy to cover larger, unintentional discharges. Note that the Baltic Water Agency would adjust fees charged in accordance with ship size and weather conditions.

4.7 Different types of environmental resources

The term 'natural resources' is applied to a wide variety of resources that are directly or indirectly employed in the production process. The classical economists – Smith, Ricardo, Mill, etc. spoke of three groups of resources: land, labor and capital. 'Land' was the term given to natural resources that yielded a continual flow of services required by the production processes. In theory, this flow was not reduced by the processes, as the amount of 'land' available at the start of the year was identical to that available at the end. However, this concept of land is not broad enough to include all of the natural and environmental resources that were presented in figure 1. Neither are the usual classification of 'depletable' and 'non-depletable' resources analytically practical as all resources are, in the final analysis, depletable. A more useful classification is based on the growth capacity of a resource, or the possibility of including it in the price system.

One basis for classification would thus be a resource's ability to renew or reproduce itself. This assumes that at any moment there is a given supply of different resources that can either increase or decrease, or only decrease. In either case, these resources yield a certain amount of services per unit time. Such resources may be called inventory resources, and may or may not be renewable. Those that are renewable have a natural rate of growth and yield a continual stream of resource. The non-renewable or non-reproducible resources have totally different characteristics. Any depletion of the inventory stock necessarily reduces the resource's availability. This was not the case with the former as long as the depletion was less than growth rate.[7] When used in a production process, non-

[7] Growth refers only to physical growth; note that this is different from an increased availability due to improved production techniques.

renewable resources undergo such physical and chemical changes that they are effectively destroyed. Fossil fuels and iron ore are examples. Most of the anti-growth debate has centered on just this type of resource. But note that the materials, which change in form, do not really disappear. Some of them are transformed to manufactured goods, while others become wastes that are returned to nature. Indeed, even manufactured goods eventually become waste and are returned to nature.

There are other resources, available in given quantities, that are not affected by the rate at which they are exploited. We shall call such resources capital resources. These yield continuous services and can be used without limit; one period's use does not affect the next period's use. Of course, these resources are limited in each period: one cannot exploit a 40 mph wind if its only blowing at 20 mph. Examples here are sun, wind, and tide energy. While the private and social costs for these resources do not differ – both are close to zero – the huge investment costs needed to tame these forces limit their use. Once such investments are made, fuel costs are zero.

A final basis for classifying natural resources is their marketability; some can be sold on the market at a positive price, while others cannot. Thus wind energy cannot be marketed other than indirectly via the price of land in windy places; in fact the only capital resource that can be marketed seems to be land. Further, inventory resources may or may not be encompassed by the market. Fossil fuels and iron ore are examples of the former, fish and water examples of the latter.

It is this non-marketable group of inventory resources that are at the center of environmental care issues. But even marketable inventory resources cause problems since the market price is usually a short term price, and futures markets for periods beyond a year are very uncertain. In this sense, the market mechanism for these inventory resources is not all inclusive even though ownership rights and current prices can be established.

4.8 Non-renewable natural resources and long-run economic development

The issue of non-renewable natural resources raises a number of questions in economic analysis. The two most interesting are as follows:

(1) Are these resources really limited in the sense that all production will become, if not impossible, at least extremely difficult in say

one or two hundred years? There are, in turn, two aspects to this issue: Are these resources limited in a scientific or an economic sense? What effect will the increased scarcity of these resources have on technological development?

(2) How can society weigh today's welfare against the welfare of future generations? Can the market only solve short term allocation problems, implying that all long run planning must be done by other institutions? What exactly does an optimal allocation between today's and future generations actually mean given that these individuals will never meet?

Many of these issues have been raised during the last few years' often pessimistic discussions on the limits to growth. We shall not thoroughly examine all the issues, but since discussions of environmental care are often coupled to the problems of non-reproducible natural resources we feel that we should present an economic analysis of the issues. The coupling of these two topics is often misleading as well as inappropriate. The question of the limited availability of these resources is one of optimal allocation over a long period, while the optimal allocation of environmental resources concerns but a single time period, and is thus not directly connected to the growth process.

Inventory natural resources that are non-renewable do create a problem for long term development. The implication of this statement can be best understood by studying a simple example of one such resource, oil. We assume that the total amount of oil is given, and ignore the possibility of technical advance. Given these extreme assumptions, one can demonstrate that there is some long run equilibrium characterized by an equal per capita income per period until the end of the planning period, whether that be 10, 30 or 300 years in the future. The optimal strategy will be given by

$\max \int_{0}^{N} f(x)dx$, where N is the planning horizon. The answer changes

as N grows, but with a given N we do not consider what happens in year $N+1$.

If the planning period is continuously extended further into the future, equilibrium per capita income will fall steadily, and each new generation will accuse the preceding one of consuming too much of that precious oil. Note that this development is rather different from the picture painted by the doomsday prophets who picture a rapid decrease in per capita income rather than a gradual one.

However, rather than further expanding the model, let us critically examine its assumptions and, at the same time, relate our discussion to the recent oil 'crisis'. First of all, the relevant issue is not one of a single non-renewable resource: different types of non-renewable resource such as the different fossil fuels or iron ore are used in different production processes and the substitution of one for another depends mostly on current prices and scarcities. The current high rate of growth in energy consumption has been coupled with a long term fall in energy prices. Thus the increase in room temperature in Swedish flats from 17° to 23° during the past few decades has been the result of falling prices and increasing incomes. The increasing scarcity of oil results in higher prices which provide the incentive for the adoption of a number of energy conserving measures: one can always rely on known techniques such as woolen sweaters, more blankets and better insulation. The debate on future growth has tended to ignore such price and substitution effects.

This leads us to a rather interesting theorem: suppose a market economy where individuals and firms make full plans for the future; the rate of price increases in an inventory type non-renewable natural resource will never exceed the rate of interest. For if one expected its price to rise by more than the rate of interest, it would be more profitable to buy and store the resource than to invest elsewhere. For example, to buy up oil for future delivery would be a more attractive alternative than an investment paying only the rate of interest. Such purchases would increase the price of future contracts until the return on them was equal to the rate of interest.

The main objection raised to this line of reasoning is that market behavior is too myopic to be able to efficiently allocate resources in this manner: the planning period for both individuals and firms is much shorter than that required for such optimal solutions to be realizable. This myopia, claim the opponents, leads to repeated short run crises and sudden price increases. However, even this myopia does not justify rationing non-renewable resources so that future needs can be met. Even if the market cannot adequately take future generations' claims into consideration, surely the political system must be able to do so. If, from the politicians' point of view, the prices of raw materials are too low in relation to future demand, these prices can be brought into line by appropriate taxes. This approach through the market system will be much more efficient than rationing. Actually, this is the same problem as taxes versus regulations that we studied previously, except that we are now concerned with allocation over time rather than space.

There are however, valid objections that can be raised against this solution. The raw materials market is dominated by monopolistic firms which tend to drive up prices by restraining production. As the difference between these prices and those which would obtain under perfect competition can be considered as private taxes, it seems difficult to support a policy aimed against these firms' production levels at the same time as we feel that we are consuming excess amounts of fossil fuel.

But there is no real guarantee that political decisions stemming from democratic procedures will have a planning period longer than the market. After all, in democratic voting procedures the votes of all citizens, the young as well as the old, have the same weight, while the market, given certain ideal conditions, will weigh each person's vote with the present value of his future income: that is, the young will have a larger say in the planning process than the old.

Moreover, in a market economy, even unanticipated price changes will provide an incentive to alter behavior in a desirable direction. First of all, increasing raw materials' prices encourages the substitution of other materials or resources for those whose prices are increasing. The price system is a rather ingenious device whose signals contain information on relative scarcity and operate to allocate resources to those industries whose comparative advantages are greatest – that is, where it would be the most expensive to replace them. For example, increased oil prices will first affect residential heating while the petrochemical industry will still find it profitable to use oil even if these prices increase greatly.

Secondly, the size of today's known or estimated reserves is not technically but economically determined. Increases in oil or iron ore prices lead to increased prospecting for these resources. It is perhaps optimal not to have reserves in excess of the requirements for the next two or three decades, as it usually requires a period of this length for newly opened oil fields or ore mines to produce profitably (unless one is to reduce the return to previous investments in the field). More than likely, we have today a greater number of oil-drilling projects than is optimal. A rational world economy would first pump up all oil in Saudi Arabia before turning to the North Sea fields.

Finally, a price increase for a scarce raw material provides an incentive for innovation and technical improvement which economizes on the use of that resource. Higher oil prices caused by decreasing supplies lead to the development of techniques to use oil in a more efficient manner (better insulation, more efficient motors, etc.) as well as to the development of alternative sources of power (breeder reactors or fusion devices).

4.9 Renewable resources and their uses

As with non-renewable resources, inventory natural resources that
are renewable are not easily allocated in an optimal manner by the
market. The issues at hand, however, are not identical since the
renewable natural resources produce a flow of services in any one
time period that may be consumed without endangering future
consumption so long as present use does not exceed the net renewal
of the resource during the period under consideration. However, it is
possible to exploit these resources to such an extent that the resource
may cease to exist. Thus the question of a depletion of these
resources has a much more immediate relevance than in the case for
non-renewable ones. A main problem here concerns those animal
and plant species for which extinction is a real threat. Note that
extinction is a truly irreversible process of an entirely different nature
from that in the preceding discussion where the availability of non-
renewable resources was more an economic than a physiological
question.

We shall address ourselves to the question of the optimal allocation of such resources through time and to the ability of the market
to resolve this allocation issue. Is the market, in this case as well, a
mechanism for short but not long term adjustments which may well
allow certain species to become extinct?

As already stated free goods are liable to over-exploitation.
Nature's own waste processors, micro-organisms, are such an
example. The result can well be that the absorptive capacity of a
body of water is at least temporarily destroyed. The issue becomes
clearer if we choose another organism (a renewable inventory
resource) such as fish or whales that lack owners and thus lack
market prices to regulate their use. While assigning ownership rights
to these resources will not necessarily guarantee their survival, the
probability of a non-optimal exploitation rate is less than if they were
free public goods.

An inventory resource such as whales will, if left undisturbed in its
element, tend towards an equilibrium position with zero net growth
in any given period. The introduction of human exploitation then
raises the question of the size of the optimal catch. However, this
optimum is not only determined by biological growth capacity, but
also by economic considerations such as hunting costs and the return
to employed resources in other fields, that is, the rate of interest. One
possible optimal catch is what biologists usually call the maximum
sustainable yield, which is obtained by reducing the size of the stock

from its natural equilibrium to the point where net growth is maximized. A stock of this size can also be considered in equilibrium as long as the annual catch is equal to the net growth. However, the maximum sustainable yield is derived from biological considerations alone. As the actual fishing activities imply real costs in the traditional economic sense, it seems most plausible that fishermen would seek to maximize profits rather than catches. If one assumes that costs are inversely proportional to the size of the stock and that the price per unit catch is constant, the economically optimal catch is less than the maximum sustainable yield and thus the stock is larger than that which would maintain this maximum yield. With no restrictions placed on these activities, and assuming that the fish or whales are free goods, any profit earned by fishermen will encourage people to enter this field, a trend that will continue until this profit disappears, that is, until total costs are equal to total revenue. The size of the stock in this economic equilibrium will probably be less than that corresponding to the maximum yield. It is possible that the lack of private ownership results in an activity level that will reduce the stock below the level necessary for its survival, and, with its natural ability to reproduce destroyed, the species will die out. Given private ownership of the stock and thus the right to limit the number of fishermen and the size of the catch, the chances of over-exploitation are greatly reduced, but do not disappear entirely, as the size of the catch under these conditions will depend on the return that the capital invested in fishing could earn in other sectors. The central issue here is how much of the stock should be left to give future returns and how much should be used for current ones. As the stock yields returns by reproducing itself, this question becomes whether this rate of reproduction is sufficient: is this rate the same as that rate of return in the rest of the economy? Thus the dynamic equilibrium obtains when the whale owners are indifferent between killing a whale and letting it reproduce itself. One of the main factors that determine this equilibrium is the rate at which one discounts future returns to the stock. If the rate of interest in other sectors is exceptionally high it is conceivable, given a whale's slow rate of reproduction, that an optimal strategy would be to kill all living whales and invest the resulting income in other sectors. Thus it is conceivable that species will become extinct even if they are privately owned.

However, this conclusion is based purely on economic considerations. If society values whales in themselves, either for the pleasure given by seeing them free in sea or for purely scientific reasons, then it is always possible to protect them by taxes or by regulation. Such measures are in principle the same as those discussed earlier in connection with traditional environmental care issues such as sulphur and phosphorus discharges.

4.10 Summary

In this final chapter we have briefly discussed a variety of special problems connected with the formulation of an optimal environmental policy within an expanded perspective. We earlier confined ourselves mainly to pollution problems restricted to a limited area such as a region or a country, where various means of controlling pollution are available. However, many environmental problems are transnational, which gives rise to certain problems when attempting to formulate an optimal policy. One conclusion which can be drawn from the analysis is that there are no standard methods such as regulation or charges that can be effective without some complementary agreements between the countries that are affected by the pollution. Such agreements do exist but seem to be very easy to break because of the difficulties of monitoring the pollutants and the limited legal possibilities for punishing the polluters. Another conclusion from this chapter is that there are no gains from changing the economic system or the method of organizing the economy, since environmental problems are not connected to a particular economic system but to the level of industrialization. In the last section of the chapter we discuss the commonly raised question of limits to growth and future levels of welfare. For this kind of analysis it is convenient to make a distinction between non-renewable and renewable natural resources. The problems of allocation for both are discussed. According to this mechanism, demand and supply tend to equilibrium through changes in market prices, substitution and innovation. This kind of self-regulation however fails to work in the allocation of the renewable resources because of the public character of many of these resources. But an important conclusion is that it does not seem to be a sufficient condition for an optimal policy to make the public resource private. It is also necessary to take into consideration the rate of reproduction and the rate of return to other resources in the economy.

Bibliography

General references

Barkley, P., Seckler, D., *Economic Growth and Environmental Decay: The Solution Becomes the Problem*, New York 1972.

Baumol, W. J., Oates, W. E., *The Theory of Environmental Policy*, New Jersey 1975.

Bolwig, N. G., 'A Survey of the Economic Theory of Pollution', *Nationaløkonomisk Tidsskrift*, 1971.

Commoner, B., *The Closing circle*, Stockholm 1972.

Crocker, T. D., Rogers, A. J., *Environmental Economics*, Hinsdale 1971.

Dolan, E., *TANSTAAFL: The Economic Strategy for Environmental Crisis*, New York 1971.

'Environmental Economics', *The Swedish Journal of Economics*, vol 73, 1971, No. 1 March.

Freeman, M., Haveman, R., Kneese, A. V., *The Economics of Environmental Policy*, New York 1973.

Goldman, M., *Ecology and Economics: Controlling Pollution in the 1970s*, Englewood Cliffs 1972.

Herfindahl, O. C., *Economic Theory of National Resources*, Ohio 1974.

Jarrett, H. (ed), *Environmental Quality in a Growing Economy*, Baltimore 1966.

Kneese, A. V., Bower, B. T., (eds), *Environmental Quality Analysis: Theory and Method in the Social Sciences*, Baltimore 1972.

Kneese, A. V., Bower, B. T., *Managing Water Quality: Economics, Technology, Institutions*, Baltimore 1968.

OECD, *Environmental Damage Costs*, Paris 1974.

OECD, *The Polluter Pays Principle*, Paris 1975.

OECD, *Economic Implications of Pollution Control*, Paris 1974.

OECD, *Problems of Environmental Economics*, Paris 1972.

Ramsay, W., Anderson, C., *Managing the Environment: An Economic Primer*, New York 1972.

Seneca, J., Taussig, M., *Environmental Economics*, New Jersey 1974.

Thompson, D., *The Economics of Environmental Protection*, Massachusetts 1973.

Ward, B., Dubos, R., *Only One Earth*, Harmondsworth 1972.
Victor, P., *Economics of Pollution*, London 1972.

Chapter 1

Dales, J. H., *Pollution, property and prices*, Toronto 1970.
Haavelmo, T., *Some observation on Welfare and Economic Growth*, Oslo 1971.
Kneese, A. V., Ayres, R. U., Dárge, R. C., *Economics and the Environment: A Materials Balance Approach*, Washington 1970.
Kneese, A. V., 'Background for the Economic Analysis of Environmental Pollution', *The Swedish Journal of Economics*, March 1971.

Chapter 2

Bohm, P., *Social Efficiency: A Concise Introduction to Welfare Economics*, London 1974.
Johansen, L., *Offentlig økonomikk*, Oslo 1967.
Koopmans, Tj., *Three Essays on the State of Economic Science*, New York 1957.
Musgrave, R., *The Theory of Public Finance*, New York 1959.
Mäler, K. G., *Environmental Economics: A Theoretical Inquiry*, Baltimore 1974.

Chapter 3

Clawson, M., Knetsch, J., *Economics of Outdoor Recreation*, Baltimore 1966.
Davidson, P., Adams, G., Seneca, J., 'The Social Value of Water Recreational Facilities Resulting from an Improvement in Water Quality: The Delaware Estuary', *The Journal of Economic Studies*, July 1968.
Fulcher, M., Burton, T., 'Measurement of Recreations Benefits – A Survey', *The Journal of Economic Studies*, July 1968.
Jordening, D. L., *Estimating Water Quality Benefits*, EPA 600/5-74-014. Washington 1974.
Knetsch, J., Davis, R., 'Comparisons of Methods for Recreation Evaluation', in Kneese, A. V., and Smith S. C. (eds), *Water Research*, Baltimore 1966.
Reiling, S. S., Gibbs, K. C., Stoevener, H. H., *Economic Benefits from an improvement in Water Quality*, EPA-K5-73-008 Washington 1973.
Sulfur in air and precipitation, Sweden's case study for the United Nations conference on the human environment, Stockholm 1971.
Environmental Quality, the second annual report of the council on environmental quality, Washington August 1971.
Sweden's national report to the United Nations on the human environment, Stockholm 1971.

Chapter 4

Baumol, W., *Environmental Protection, International Spillovers and Trade*, (Wicksell Lectures 1971) Uppsala 1971.

Beckermann, W., *In Defence of Economic Growth*, London 1974.

Clark, C., 'The Economics of Overexploitation', *Science* 181.

Dahmén, E., 'Environmental Control and Economic Systems', *Swedish Journal of Economics*, March 1971.

Goldman, M., *The Spoils of Progress — Environmental Pollution in the Soviet Union*, Massachusetts 1972.

Gordon, R., 'A Reinterpretation of the Pure Theory of Exhaustion', *Journal of Political Economy*, 1967.

Hannesson, R., *Economics of Fisheries: Some Problems of Efficiency*, Lund 1974.

Hodson, H., *The Diseconomics of Growth*, London 1972.

Hotelling, H., 'The Economics of Exhaustible Resources', *Journal of Political Economy*, April 1931.

Linbeck, A., 'Ekonomiska System', *Ekonomisk Debatt*, 1973.

Meadows, D., *The Limits to Growth*, London 1972.

Mesarovic, M., Pestel, E., *Mankind at the Turning Point*, London 1975.

Mishan, E., *The Costs of Economic Growth*, London 1967.

The book deals with the problems involved in trying to manage the environment. Its main aim is to depict the control of the environment as an economic issue, and to show what economic policies should be developed to improve environmental quality. The main ideas of welfare economics necessary for this purpose are introduced and the essential concept of the common property resource is explained. This concept and its associated idea of market failure provide the basic framework used to analyse environmental problems and policies in the book.

A major part of the book is devoted to employing these analytic tools on a series of policy problems and their solutions. Amongst these are the estimation of benefits from outdoor recreation, disposable versus returnable containers, chemical pollution of water by detergents, air pollution, lead poisoning and the general work environment.

Another major part of the book is devoted to regional and international aspects of environmental protection, discussing the institutions required and the consequences for international trade. This broader view of the environmental problem is also demonstrated in the discussion of the possible relation between environmental quality and the nature of the economic system; for example, does a centralised economy provide the chance for greater safeguards against pollution?

This textbook provides a thorough coverage of environmental economics and demands prior knowledge of no more than introductory economics.

£2.50 net in UK

Cover design by Ken Vail

Also issued in hard covers

CAMBRIDGE UNIVERSITY PRESS

0 521 29182 8

HANDEL
AND
HIS AUTOGRAPHS

A. HYATT KING

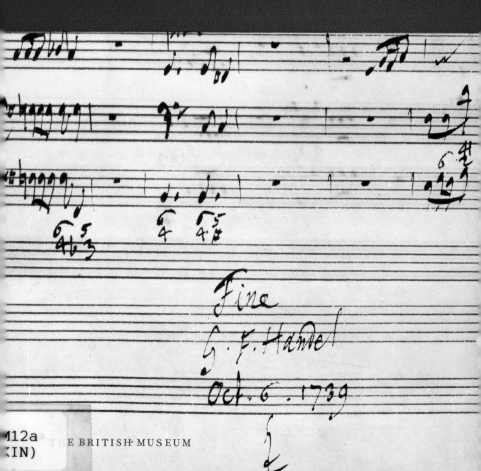